MW00712502

WHAT OTHER REALLY IM}
SAYING ABOUT THIS BOOK!

"Patrick has not only delivered great programs, full of music, humor, and insight, but he has also gotten to the core of what serving customers means. The humanness and truth he uses to simultaneously make light of and focus seriously on the business of customer relations will show all in his audience that they can make a real difference. Timing, style, and heart are essential in great customer service and Patrick tactfully uses all three in his comedy and in his music. His guitar skills are pretty good too."

Simon Nance
Manager - Learning & Development, STIHL Inc.

"The Pancake Principle is not just a book about how to succeed in sales, but how to succeed in life. Brilliant! ".

David W. Westcott
2013 Chairman, National Automobile Dealers
Association of America

THE PANCAKE PRINCIPLE

Patrick Henry

SEVENTEEN STICKY WAYS TO MAKE YOUR CUSTOMERS FLIP FOR YOU

© 2013 Patrick Henry
All Rights Reserved.

No part of this publication may be reproduced, stored in a retrieval system, or
transmitted, in any form or by any means, electronic, mechanical, photocopying,
recording, or otherwise, without the written permission of the author.

First published by Dog Ear Publishing
4010 W. 86th Street, Ste H
Indianapolis, IN 46268
www.dogearpublishing.net

ISBN: 978-1-4575-1579-8

This book is printed on acid-free paper.

Printed in the United States of America

Contents

ACKNOWLEDGEMENTS

I was once told to "choose your mentors well, and thank them often." I want to take this opportunity to acknowledge and thank not only my mentors but some special people in my life who make it fun, interesting, and worth living.

First and foremost, I'd like to mention my family. My wife, Lesley, who makes life worth the journey. She is the love of my life ... period. My kids, Meredith, Robert, and Jack, who not only occupy most of my time but my heart as well. My mother, Merrilyn Henry, whom I love and admire more than any woman I've ever known (my wife not included). My brother, Brent ,who continues to impress me with his success in business and his willingness to step out and take on a new challenge. My wonderful in-laws Tom, Toni, and brother-in-law Andy. I'd also like to mention my aunt Mary Henry, who I've learned is an amazing lady. Finally, I'd like to mention my father, the late Robert Henry, who lived his life setting the example that I strive to live up to.

I am blessed to know some terrific professional speakers and writers. My involvement in the National Speakers Association and the Carolinas chapter of NSA has given me access to the expertise of great speakers and thought leaders and also great friendships. My biggest heroes and friends in this business are Jeanne Robertson, Al Walker, Nido Qubein, Ty Boyd, Scott McKain, Patricia Fripp, Jim Cathcart, Don

Hutson, Mike Frank, Jane Jenkins Herlong, Jeffrey Gitomer, and many others. I also want to mention some special speaker buds who help and encourage me continually: Theo Androus, Thom Singer, Alan Berg, Robert Fishbone, Jana Stanfield, Wally Adamchick, Denise Ryan, and Michelle Joyce. They are terrific master minders and always have great friendship and advice. I know I am leaving important people off, and I apologize from the bottom of my soul, but rest assured that I remembered you as soon as I sent in the manuscript. I want to also mention my buddies James Gurule and Brian Hunt. I have wonderful friends from my past, but these two are the ones I seem to keep dragging into the next phase of my life.

Thanks to SiriusXM Radio for continuing to play me on Blue Collar Radio and the Family Comedy channel. It never gets old.

PREFACE

For ten years, I lived in Nashville, Tennessee, as a professional songwriter and musician, where I wrote songs for a Music City publishing company. In addition to writing songs, I toured the country, playing music with various bands in venues ranging from clubs to casinos to state fairs. There was a stretch in the midnineties where I was a regular performer at a little place called the Bluebird Café. If you have heard of the Bluebird, then you know that it is a world-famous songwriters' joint that has hosted some of the world's best songwriters. I was able to charm my way onto the stage, despite *NOT* being one of the world's best songwriters. I usually played with the same three people, and we performed what is called a writer's round. We sat in a circle in the middle of the room, and the audience crowded around tables jammed in all around us. The Bluebird seated around eighty people and usually had twenty or so more standing around the walls. The intimacy of the Bluebird invited the songwriters to not only play their songs but to also tell the stories about how the song came to be, which made the audience feel like they were a part of an intimate backstage conversation. I wrote really good songs … but if you want to make it big in Nashville, you have to write really *great* songs. In order to keep up with my coperformers, I crafted funny and poignant stories to introduce my songs, and I became known as much for my stories as I was for the songs I wrote.

After a show one evening, a man approached me and said that he enjoyed the show and would like for me to perform for the insurance company he worked for at their annual meeting being held in Nashville. I told him that I would be delighted to, and since in those days I happily played for free, I didn't even discuss payment. I put together an hour of funny songs and stories and even wove in a little message to leave them feeling good. After the show, my host approached me.

"Patrick," he said, "I sure enjoyed your speech."

I thought, "Speech? What's he talking about? I'm not a speaker. I'm a songwriter, a composer, an artiste."

He then handed me a check for $500.

I looked him square in the eye and said, "I'm glad you enjoyed that speech." A career was born.

In the early days, I simply wanted to entertain audiences, but as my career has continued to evolve, I've come to realize that the same key elements of success that make great artists and musicians great are the same key elements that make a great attorney or HR professional shine in their fields. I've discovered that the delivery of that message with music, humor, and stories is not only unique but worth paying for. I use analogies of musical artists and stories from the Nashville music scene simply because it is my frame of reference and the lens through which I view the world. I hope you enjoy the book but, more importantly, use it to help sculpt your frame of reference so all of your customers, clients, and coworkers will sing your praises.

INTRODUCTION

The Pancake Principle: Like making perfect pancakes, creating an extraordinary customer experience requires preparation, skill, focus, patience, and timing.

Nothing says home to me like the smell of pancakes. I can almost taste the sticky-sweet memories of waking up on Saturday mornings as a child to the smell of pancakes being cooked on the stove. My mother made it look so easy. The way she could make every single pancake look exactly the same both in size and color was nothing less than awesome. Like a conductor leading an orchestra, she would bring the kitchen to order with a flick of her wooden spoon, evoking a harmonious blend of texture, taste, and aroma. I learned a lot about life from my father, but my ability to make the perfect pancake is attributed to my mother.

Saturday mornings in the Henry house can best be described as elegantly chaotic. Saturday mornings unveil cartoons blaring in the background, the rich aroma of K-Cups pouring from the Keurig, and the sounds of screaming children trying to gain purchase in the ever-present battle for the remote control. Most might fail to see the beauty in a stage set with such discord, but amid the noise stands an asylum of calm, an island of focused serenity untouched by the waves of

1

pandemonium. That island is me, dear old dad, making pancakes. Like Brigadoon emerging from the mist, I materialize in the kitchen once a week to calm the masses with sticky stacks of buttery, sweet pancakes dripping with syrup.

The key to making a perfect pancake is focus. Regardless of what is occurring around you, your focus must remain on the pancake in the middle of the pan. Sure, there are other tasks to attend to (pouring coffee, frying bacon, drop-kicking kids across the room), but the forefront of your mind must be occupied by one thing: the pancake in the pan. If neglected for a minute or not turned at the proper time, then the pancake can be ruined, and you will have to begin again.

What, you ask, does making pancakes have to do with growing a business, managing a team, creating an extraordinary customer experience, or living a life of excellence and abundance? *The Pancake Principle* is about a process of achievement that's predicated by certain core fundamentals. Most people strive for prosperity and accomplishment, and, like in making pancakes, there is a recipe to guide your actions. It is, however, more than simply following steps. You must apply the necessary talent and skill, or you will find yourself with burned, tasteless lumps that are a far cry from what you originally set out to create. The following pages will share seventeen sticky-sweet ingredients that will enable you to create the perfect pancake. For you, the perfect pancake might mean momentum in your business, career, team, organization, or simply … your life. There are numerous ways to prepare pancakes, as there are also numerous ways to create success and prosperity. As varied as the results may be, you will find that the fundamentals required to get there are universal. Why can one man make a million dollars, lose a million dollars, and then become a millionaire again when most people can barely make ends meet? It's because that man has learned how to make a million dollars. Making perfect pancakes is simple … once you learn how.

AUTHENTICITY

*It takes courage to grow up and
become who you really are.*

—E. E. Cummings

Old-Fashioned Pancakes

1½ cups all-purpose flour
3½ teaspoons baking powder
1 tablespoon sugar
3 tablespoons melted butter
1 egg
1¼ cups of milk
PAM cooking spray

Sift together flour, baking powder, salt,
and sugar in a large bowl.
Whisk in melted butter, egg, and milk until combined.
Let batter sit for 5 minutes.
Preheat a large pan over medium-high heat.
Spray with cooking spray.
Pour batter into the hot pan, about ⅓ cup of batter for each
pancake. Cook for 2-3 minutes, until bubbles appear on the
sides and center of each pancake.
Flip and cook until golden, about 1-2 minutes.

I love country music. Ever since I was eight years old and first heard Charlie Daniels sing "The Devil Went Down to Georgia," I've been hooked. From old Bob Wills tunes to Outlaw Country to the class of '89: Garth Brooks, Clint Black, and Alan Jackson. If you are a country music fan, you may recall the Alan Jackson song "Gone Country." What many people don't realize is that when Bob McDill wrote that song, he wrote it as a backlash against the influx of songwriters that were streaming into Nashville in the early nineties. There had been a shift in the music scene. Eighties heavy metal had become a parody of itself, grunge was still fringe music, and rap had become too scary for middle-class white kids. It didn't help that the California earthquake of 1994 scared the hell out of West Coast songwriters who migrated east for more stable geography. I'm not sure who first said that "nature abhors a vacuum," but I feel fairly confident that whoever it was wasn't referring to the American suburban music scene ... or was he? In the late eighties and early nineties, the ground had been sown for the rebirth of country music—fun music that middle-class America could dance to. The country music industry at the time was still considered backward. Albums were being produced for less than $50,000, unlike their rock and pop counterparts that were costing hundreds of thousands if not millions of dollars to produce. It wasn't until Jimmy Bowen, Garth Brooks's producer, came to town and dragged Nashville kicking and screaming into the big leagues that the world began to take notice. All of a sudden, everyone with guitars in their laps and songs in their hearts felt like they could make it rich as Nashville songwriters—and some of them could. It was easy to spot poseurs in those days. If their snakeskin boots had matching snakeskin belts or their jeans had pleats, it was probably safe to assume that they were not straight off of the ranch. Authenticity is hard to come by, and when a truly authentic artist hits the scene, history is made. George Strait has been in the business for over thirty-five years with fifty-nine number-one singles. He is the real deal. He is a Texas rancher who would be as comfortable in the saddle on a horse as he would be singing in front of sixty thousand people in Cowboys Stadium. He has lived much of what he sings about. Hip-hop is a multibillion dollar industry due, in part, to the authenticity of its artists. A poseur in the rap world is easily unmasked and quickly discarded.

As a songwriter, I tried to write songs that would appeal to the country singers of the day. Although I had a few songs recorded by various artists, I never had that big hit that I was so desperately seeking. Looking back, I finally admit that it was because I was being inauthentic. I was trying to plug into the Nashville formula. The songs being recorded were "hooky" songs that spoke of love, loss, and line dancing. The problem was that there were so many people who could do that better than I could. I eventually began to develop a bit of a reputation around town for my funny songs. These were the songs that I had no intention of pitching because they did not fit the Nashville formula. The irony is that now, years after I have moved away from Nashville and the country music business, those same funny songs are being played daily on the SiriusXM Radio Family Comedy channel and the Blue Collar

Radio channel, and at the end of each quarter, I get a sticky-sweet little check. Once you present your authentic self to the world, people respond.

I was recently struck by a post that I read on a LinkedIn group for professional speakers and entertainers. It read, "Clean comedian for corporate, government, or personal events. Contact me for rates and availability." I was intrigued not because I am looking for a corporate comic but because I wanted to see the face of the person who would break etiquette and blatantly advertise on LinkedIn. I googled the name and found a YouTube clip of a comedy show that he did a couple of years ago. "Clean comedian" is how this person branded himself, and twenty-eight seconds into his act, he dropped the F-bomb. *The F-bomb!* Now don't get me wrong; I am not easily offended by profanity as long as it's not around my kids, but I *am* offended by a misleading branding statement. If you say your book is a best seller, you'd better not mean within your mother's Bible study. If you say you are the toughest man in the world, there better be a line of broken and battered bodies littering your wake, and if you say you are a clean comedian, then you'd better not drop the F-bomb. If I were to have a conversation with this gentleman and express my opinion, he would probably tell me that he modifies his language based on the event, or he may just tell me to F off. I would then tell him, "You can't call yourself a vegetarian and have your tofu wrapped in bacon." Unlike in years past, we no longer have control over our brand. Major companies like Nike, Apple, and McDonald's spend millions of dollars creating a branding statement which is nothing more than four or five words that come to mind when you hear a product name. Nike = swoosh, sports, running, football. Apple = Mac, sleek, fast, elite. McDonald's = easy, tasty, kids, cheap. For years, corporations were able to control their brands with advertisements and commercials. This is no longer the case. Thanks to social media and YouTube, the control of our brand has transferred to the consumer. If I receive bad customer service, I tell my online community. If I do it in a funny or interesting way, then it will ripple into their communities. Videos of me speaking and performing are all over YouTube and Vimeo. Some were put up by me and some by others. Because the Internet provides immediate access into our brand, there is a transparency between us and the customer that has never before existed. The best way for us to promote and protect our brand is to simply *be the brand.*

As a professional speaker and writer, the outcome generated by my message is as important to me as the income it generates. Authenticity is paramount to the acceptance of my message as it is with any speaker. I recently attended a conference of professional speakers in Dallas, Texas, and was thrilled to hear my buddy Randy Gage speak. Randy told a group of around three hundred speakers that if you were to visit any of our websites, you would see what our topics are, what our backgrounds and credentials are, and where we went to college. Heck, you would probably even read how many kids we have. He then told us that rarely will you see on a website the speaker's perspective or point of view. Randy said that he feels it is important for an audience to know what we, as speakers, believe. That statement resonated with me, so I now begin all of my speeches with the following statement.

> I believe that success is your fault. I believe that failure is your fault. I believe attitude is everything. I believe conventions should be as entertaining as they are informative. I believe attitude is contagious, funny is funner, and social media is the best thing to happen to customer service since the paper receipt. I believe people want to do business with friends, people are more productive when working with nice people, and civility is good for business. I believe the difference between good and great is measured in inches, you should tell your wife and children you love them every single day, and that one good person can change the world.

What do you believe? What are your purpose, core values, and message? What makes you pump your fist in the air and shout hallelujah? More importantly, do you communicate your authentic self to your customers, team, or community? Once you begin to do that, you will begin to develop an honest relationship with those whom you serve that will lead to more business, better employee relationships, and a healthier work environment. People will buy our products, but they will buy into our beliefs.

Side note: I write this the day after Chick-fil-A appreciation day. Chick-fil-A president Dan Cathy made polarizing comments that led to thousands of customers lining up at Chick-fil-A stores around the country to buy fried chicken sandwiches. Why? Although this is a divisive issue, if we look at it from thirty thousand feet, we will see a company that has a history of promoting its beliefs (right or wrong), and the public has responded vigorously.

What do you believe? I believe it is important to be able to articulate what you do and what you believe in one sentence. For the purposes of this chapter, let's uncover your core beliefs as they relate to your business, mission, or purpose.

I believe _____
I believe _____
I believe _____
I believe _____
I believe _____
I believe _____
I believe _____
I believe _____

String them together, and you have a belief statement. Live it.

ASSOCIATION

A man only learns in two ways, one by reading, and the other by association with smarter people.

—Will Rogers

Lemon Poppy Seed Pancakes

1½ cups all-purpose flour
3½ teaspoons baking powder
1 tablespoon sugar
3 tablespoons melted butter
1 egg
1¼ cups of milk
PAM cooking spray

Sift together flour, baking powder, salt,
and sugar in a large bowl.
Stir 1 teaspoon of finely grated lemon zest and 2 teaspoons
of poppy seeds into dry ingredients.
Whisk in melted butter, egg, and milk until combined.
Let batter sit for 5 minutes.
Preheat a large pan over medium-high heat.
Spray with cooking spray.
Pour batter into the hot pan, about ⅓ cup of batter for each
pancake. Cook for 2-3 minutes, until bubbles appear on the
sides and center of each pancake.
Flip and cook until golden, about 1-2 minutes.

I am a Southerner. I grew up in Alabama, and my roots are known to show from time to time. However, not many of my friends know that I was born in Silver Spring, Maryland. For the first four years of my life, my father worked as a lobbyist in Washington DC. We were the only non-Jewish family living in a predominantly Jewish neighborhood, so from an early age, this Southern Baptist Alabama boy developed a taste for Jewish cuisine. Lox, bagels, chopped liver, and gefilte fish were common fare when I was visiting with the Liebermans or the Rosenthals. Years later when I was living in Nashville, Tennessee, as a single musician, I befriended an older Jewish woman who lived in a small house in my neighborhood in Hillsboro Village. She was trying to mow her lawn one day and seemed to be having trouble, so I helped her finish. She invited me into her home for a glass of iced tea. She shared with me pictures of her children and grandchildren and even a picture of her ex-husband. "May God rest his soul … soon" (her quote). A beautiful menorah was displayed on her mantle, so I told her of my early years in the all-Jewish neighborhood outside of Washington DC. She said we were the "token gentiles." We came to an agreement on that day. I would mow her yard in exchange for her homemade chopped liver. Music City had never seen such a deal and probably never will again. I'll never forget the advice Mrs. Frank gave me one afternoon over lemonade.

She said, "It is just as easy to marry smart and beautiful as it is to marry dumb and plain." I married a smart and beautiful woman, and I thank God every day that my wife never met Mrs. Frank for fear that she would have done the same.

Mrs. Frank was right. It is just as easy to marry smart and beautiful as it is to marry dumb and plain. It is also as easy if not easier to put talented and motivated people on your team as it is slackers. My good friend and former bandmate Ben plays drums for one of the biggest country music stars in the business. I remember when he got the gig. He and I were waiting tables at Jack Russell's restaurant, which was a hidden little café known for its pecan-crusted catfish and foul-tempered waiters. He came into work one day and said that he had an audition with a new act on Arista Records. We all felt like Ben would get the gig because he was an excellent drummer. He was not only passionate about his instrument, but he was a professional drummer in the best sense of the word. He was trained at the Berklee College of Music in Boston and practiced a minimum of two hours a day, even when in between jobs while working as a waiter. I called him the human metronome because you could call out any number—120 beats per minute, 80 beats per minute ,or 200 beats per minute—and he could find the exact tempo from memory. He got the job and has been with this artist for almost fifteen years now. The lesson in this story is not that a great drummer got a job. The lesson lay with the artist. You see, up until this point, the artist (who will remain unnamed) had a band that consisted of buddies from high school and college. His best friend played drums for him. When he got signed to a major-label record deal, he knew that in order to be great, he had to surround himself with great musicians. Although good, his friend was not the best, and I am sure that he would have loved nothing more than to carry his buddy with him, but he knew that a mediocre drummer would have been an impediment to the band. His commitment was to greatness, and in order to achieve greatness, he had to surround himself with great players and fire his friend.

A commonality of all great people is great mentors. I have great mentors; I call them my Yodas. Nido Qubein is one of my Yodas. Dr. Qubein is a world-renowned speaker, the CEO of Great Harvest Bread Company, and the president of High Point University. I was visiting with him in his office years ago when I was a fresh-faced new college graduate. I was just starting out in my career and a little uncertain about the path I was taking. We were sitting and talking in his plush and luxurious office when he asked me to walk over to a beautiful credenza on the far side of the room. He said, "Press the button." I pressed the button, and a statue began to rise from inside the credenza. I watched as the crystal statue of three figures holding hands rose up. He told me the story of how his mother had given him the statue to always inspire and remind him to align himself with the right people. The figure in the middle represented Dr. Qubein, on his left, Albert Einstein, and on his right, Jesus Christ. The plaque at the bottom read, "If you want to be great, walk hand in hand with greatness." It could have as easily read, "If you want to have an awesome band, hire great musicians," or "If you want a profitable business, surround yourself with great salespeople." If walking hand in hand with greatness breeds greatness, then certainly the converse is true.

My father was not a farmer, although if you heard him tell the stories of picking cotton for a penny a pound after he walked up hill both ways just to understand the value of a dollar, you would think he had fertile Mississippi delta soil coursing through his veins. Whenever we moved into a new house when I was a kid, my father participated in a ritual I called the "planting of the fruit trees." My father loved nothing more than going out back and eating a peach picked off of one of his trees, so when we moved into a new house, he would plant a small orchard around the periphery of the property. When I was eight years old, we moved into a new house in Auburn, Alabama. My dad woke me up one Saturday morning, and we went to the nursery where we picked out a number of peach, pear, and plum trees for planting. When we got home, my father dug a hole around eighteen inches deep for each tree, and my job was to hold the tree steady while he shoveled in the dirt and loam around the roots and base. We watered and fertilized the trees and continued to care for them throughout the summer. I checked on the trees periodically, growing impatient at the lack of activity in the first few months. The next spring, my father woke me up early one Saturday morning and handed me a set of pruning shears. It was time to prune the peach trees. I walked into the yard and saw that some of the branches that Dad wanted removed were perfectly good. Some even had healthy buds on them. I walked back into the house a little confused and indignant. I said, "Dad, you're wrong. You don't want me to cut those branches away, do you?" He patiently told me that he was not mistaken, and I should do what he said. I'm convinced that one reason for Dad's peach trees was to have an arsenal of switches for disobedient sons. He further explained to me that peach trees are not hearty trees and if not pruned, the excess branches would choke away the sunlight from the vital parts of the tree, thus producing smaller fruit. In order to have the best fruit, it is necessary to remove the branches that choke away potential. Leave it to Dad to incorporate a life lesson into my yard work.

Sometimes there are people in our lives that act just like those branches. They clutter our work environment or our personal lives with negativity, dishonesty, or mediocrity and choke away our potential for greatness. Sometimes the best thing to do is to cut them out of our lives ... unless we are related. Then we must just suffer through holidays with them.

I used to be a smoker. It's not something that I'm proud of, and even though I quit over five years ago, there is still that rare occasion where "I sure could use a smoke." In 1996, I worked for a record label in Nashville. I worked in a department that sold music in the gift market. If you go into a gift store that is playing instrumental jazz, new age, or Appalachian mountain music, there is a good chance that we sold it. I worked with a woman named Jackie, who was also a smoker. Periodically, Jackie and I took smoke breaks with the other smokers in the office, and we huddled together like a herd of yaks, protecting each other from the elements while we got our smoke on. Jackie didn't like our boss, Debbie, one bit and used the smoke break as an opportunity to bash her. When we arrived back in the office, we not only dragged the smell of secondhand smoke with us but the negativity that

Jackie spread among our group. Jackie's negative attitude impacted the attitude of the entire office, which affected productivity. When Debbie finally understood the problem, she replaced Jackie with a cheery non-smoker.

I am a big believer in the power of association, which is why I believe that people should join clubs, groups, teams, trade associations, and community groups. In another chapter, I talk about the power of community. This chapter is about the quality of the individuals that we allow into our communities. "If you want to be great, surround yourself with greatness." Surround yourself with positive people, and separate yourself from those who bring you down.

DISTINCTION

Two roads diverged in a wood and I—
I took the one less traveled by and that
has made all the difference.

—Robert Frost

Cranberry-Ricotta Pancakes

2 cups all-purpose flour
1/4 cup sugar
2 teaspoons baking powder
1/2 teaspoon nutmeg
1/2 teaspoon cinnamon
2 cups ricotta cheese
2 teaspoons vanilla extract
6 eggs, separated
1 cup dried or frozen cranberries (thawed)

Whisk together flour, sugar, baking powder, cinnamon,
and nutmeg.
In separate bowl, beat egg whites until they are stiff.
Set aside.
In a separate bowl, whisk together, ricotta cheese,
vanilla extract, and egg yolks until blended.
Add dry mixture and stir until blended. Do not overmix.
Fold in egg whites along with cranberries.
Cook on medium-heated skillet.

It was the last flight of the evening, and I was sitting in the back of the plane, watching people. I love watching people. From the looks of my fellow passengers, it had been a long day, as there were not many smiling faces as they tried to shove oversized bags into undersized baggage compartments and make their way to their seats. We took off and eventually leveled off at cruising altitude when the flight attendants began to make their way down the aisle with the drink cart. As they got closer to where I was sitting, I began overhearing their conversation. Apparently, one of the flight attendants had some extremely rude passengers on each leg of her trip that day. She made the comment that passengers have changed since the days when she first started with the airline. She then went into a full-body spasm, which was what I could only surmise was a hot flash, and she began to vigorously fan herself. "It's so hot on this plane. Why do they do this to us? I'm miserable," she said. Then as if on cue, I counted five passengers begin to fan themselves, never looking up from what they were doing. This flight attendant had done us the courtesy of not only informing us how miserable she was but reminding us how miserable we were as well. I'm sure this flight attendant was nothing more than a person having a bad day, but it was evident to me that she had no idea the impact that her words had on the experience of everyone within earshot of her comments and anyone who asked one of us, "How was your flight?"

Are you tweetworthy? A decade ago, that question may have gotten you slapped or a least left standing by yourself at the bus stop. Now the question has a very deep and profound meaning for you and your business. When I was in college, the marketing research of the day showed that for every positive interaction a customer had, they would tell three to five people about it. For every negative experience, they would tell seven to ten people about it. Some studies showed as many as fourteen. Now thanks to social media, for every negative experience I have, I can feasibly tell seven to ten thousand people about it, and if I say it in an interesting or funny way, maybe a million. We are more connected to our communities than ever before, and with that added connectivity comes increased responsibility to our customers. My concept of tweet-worthiness was conceived long before the first poke, post, tweet, or twerp. I was sitting in the office of the A&R director of Curb Records, thinking, "This is it." This was the magical moment I'd been waiting for. This was the tipping point that I had been working toward since I first picked up a guitar, strung three chords together, and sang my own homegrown lyrics. A random encounter with Casey Kasem and a covert placement of a demo tape had led me to this moment and now, with eyes closed, I played what was sure to be Tim McGraw's next chart topper. I hit every note, added the appropriate amount of emotion and pathos. I mixed texture with melody and envisioned the excitement building two feet away in the expensive-smelling leather chair. I opened my eyes, expecting to see a face full of jubilation and awe, but was instead confronted with crossed arms and an expression devoid of emotion. I was stunned. How could this person not see the songwriting brilliance that my mother and her Bible study were so quick to acknowledge? I was then told something that changed my thinking for life: "Patrick, your songs are good. Your songs are actually really good, but hundreds of good and really good songs come through my door every week. Let me tell you about a hit song. A hit song has a quality that makes the listener get up off his butt, drive to the record store, and pay fifteen dollars just so he can hear it again. Your songs don't have that." I walked out of that office more dejected than I had ever been in my life, but looking back, I realize that it was the best business lesson I ever received.

Even though the relevance of mainstream record stores has disappeared, the relevance of that statement has not. I call it being tweetworthy. As a professional speaker, I have noticed a shift in the way the audience interacts with me. Those who introduced me used to ask the audience to turn off their cell phones out of respect for the speaker. I now ask them to turn them on. I then proceed to give them my Twitter address, @Patrickhen, and tell them to tweet about what they like or dislike about my speech. Your customers are talking about you, so why should I be different? This is representative of the shift that has taken place between the speaker and the audience. Like it or not, the audience member is now participating in the dialogue just like your customers are part of the conversation like they've never been before. I now prepare for speeches with tweetworthy moments in mind because I want my message to extend far beyond the confines of the meeting room. Are you engaging your customers, teammates, or employees in a way that will make them pick up their smartphones and tell the world how wonderful you are? Companies spend millions of dollars developing their brands. Now, thanks to the shifting conversation, the consumer is the brand builder. When you intentionally strive to not only serve those whom you are responsible to but to *wow* them, your customers, clients, and coworkers will not only sing your praises ... they'll write the song.

Three Ways to Create Tweetworthy Distinction

1. **Do the unexpected.** Observe what the competition is doing, and do something different.

2. **Provide value.** Look for opportunities to help others succeed, and you will be viewed as a resource and a person of value. That is how leaders are made, sales are closed, and customers are turned into fans

3. **Be sincere.** Praise often. Make sure you are genuine. Sincere acts of appreciation are more powerful than money and title. Treat those whom you work with, sell to, or serve the way you treat your friends, and you will be tweeted to prosperity. Just don't get your tweet caught in your twitter.

KINDNESS

If you haven't any charity in your heart,
you have the worst kind of heart trouble.

—Bob Hope

Double Chocolate Pancakes

2 eggs
1¼ cups milk
3 tablespoons melted butter
1½ cups all-purpose flour
¼ cup cocoa
2 teaspoons baking powder
¾ teaspoon salt
3 tablespoons sugar
1 cup chocolate chips

Whisk flour, salt, cocoa, baking powder, and sugar in bowl.
In another bowl, beat eggs and milk.
Stir in butter.
Blend wet and dry mixture, and then fold in chips.
Pour ⅓ cups of batter onto medium-high skillet.
When bubbles appear, flip and cook for another minute.

When I entered the Nashville music scene in 1994, it wasn't long before I was rubbing elbows with some of the biggest names in country music. Garth Brooks, Reba McEntire, Alan Jackson … I was rubbing elbows with all of them. Truth be told, it was usually when I was reaching to refill their water glasses, but every now and then, our elbows would touch. A month before, I had walked into my parents' bedroom and spoken the words that all parents long to hear from their new college graduates: "Mother, Father … thank you. Thank you for teaching me the value of hard work. Thank you for teaching me the importance of an education. Thank you for showing me how to set a goal and see it through to the end. Now I'm moving to Nashville to be a star." It didn't quite inspire the enthusiastic response that I had envisioned, but after a long discussion, my parents realized that I was determined to turn my passion into a profession.

My dad looked me in the eye and said, "Son, I'll support you … in spirit. Get a job."

So with those words of encouragement, I headed up Interstate 65 until I hit Music City.

I worked at a restaurant called the Green Hills Grille. It was a charming Southwestern-themed eatery nestled in the heart of the Green Hills area of Nashville and staffed mostly by aspiring songwriters, singers, and musicians. The joke was if you wanted a job at a restaurant in Nashville, you had to submit a three-song demo. The Green Hills Grille almost always had a line out the door, with people eagerly awaiting the spinach-and-artichoke dip, chicken salad melt, or the famous white bean soup with corn cakes. I was surprised that the restaurant did no advertising. The food at the restaurant was excellent, but the secret to their success did not lie in the taste of the food but rather with a little old woman named Mrs. Stevens. Mrs. Stevens came in every day at four o'clock and always sat at the same table, in the same chair, and order the exact same thing—a hot fudge brownie, vanilla ice cream on the side, and black coffee. We all got to know Mrs. Stevens, and when we had a chance, we stopped by her table to say hello. One afternoon, I had her table in my section, and when I saw her walk into the restaurant, I put in her order and had a cup of coffee waiting when she sat down.

As she was eating her brownie, I said, "Mrs. Stevens, we sure enjoy seeing you in here every day. You must love brownies."

She put down her fork, looked up at me, and said, "Patrick, I don't come here for the brownie. I'm here because of you … and Gail and Brigid and Jed and Doug and Steve …" To my surprise, Mrs. Stevens began to name every single server in the restaurant, and as she looked up at me, her eyes began to mist over, and she said, "Y'all make me feel so special."

Most of us remember our first day of elementary school, our first high school dance, or the first time we drove away from our house as a newly licensed driver. As vivid as those memories are in my mind, I can as vividly remember my first day of work at the Green Hills Grille. We were in a back room, taking a menu test. Brian, the general manager, walked in, spoke three words, and then left. He didn't say, "Don't be late." He didn't say, "Don't drop dishes." He simply said, *"Remember their names!"* We made it a point to get to know the customers of the Green Hills Grille, and because of that, we created an atmosphere where people felt at home. The secret to the Green Hills Grille's success was not in the food (isn't good food an expectation?)—it was that the customers felt good being there.

How do you make the people around you feel? Do your customers, team members, and employees feel valued, important, or part of the success of the group? A 2009 article in the *Harvard Business Review* written by Christine Porath and Christine Pearson gave staggering statistics on decreased workplace performance due to incivility. The article showed a 48 percent decrease in work effort, a 47 percent decreased time at work, and a 66 percent decrease in work quality. If incivility causes poor performance, then certainly creating a culture of kindness will increase performance. Maya Angelou said, "People will forget what you said. People will forget what you did, but people will never forget the way you make them feel." When you make a habit out of making the people around you feel special, you will see returns in the form of increased productivity, increased business, and increased customer loyalty.

Three Ways to Turn Customers, Clients, and Coworkers into Fans with Kindness

1. **Remember their names.** It makes them feel special and makes you look competent. Remember details of conversations you have, and recall them in follow-up correspondence.

2. **Remember their birthdays.** My father had a fraternity brother who became a successful Hollywood producer. He once told my dad that he spent $60,000 a year on flowers. He said, "They don't always remember who sent flowers, but they always remember who didn't."

3. **Remember your manners.** I was conducting interviews of my best clients, asking them why they continued to do business with me. One said, "My secretary loves you. You always call her 'ma'am.'" She was an older Southern lady who appreciated the "old school."

Name three people you will make a point to make feel special:

_____ _____ _____

EVOLUTION

*The most successful people are those
who are good at plan B.*

—James Yorke, chaos theorist

Sweet Potato Pancakes

1 cup all-purpose flour
1 cup whole-wheat flour
2 tablespoons brown sugar
4 teaspoons baking powder
1 teaspoon cinnamon
Pinch of nutmeg
2 cups milk
4 teaspoons melted butter
2 eggs
1 sweet potato cooked till tender, peeled and pureed
Maple syrup

Combine ingredients in a large bowl.
Mix together, and whisk until smooth.
Heat frying pan on medium-high temperature.
Pour ⅓ cup of batter into greased pan.
When bubbles form on surface, flip and then cook until
golden brown.

I t wasn't that long ago that I was looking at the screen of my iPhone, thinking, "How in the heck am I ever going to learn how to use this thing?" Now if I leave home without it, even while on a short trip to the grocery store, I feel like I do in that dream where I show up to school with no pants on, completely lost and vulnerable. How quickly we go from confused to competent when we give ourselves permission to begin again.

During my years in Nashville, I volunteered almost every Monday afternoon at a farm in Franklin, Tennessee. Promised Land Therapy was a group that worked with children who suffered from spinal cord injuries, cerebral palsy, or multiple sclerosis. The type of therapy administered there is called hippotherapy. The children ride horses to condition pelvic and leg muscles, and the gait of the horse simulates the walking motion of the child, thus strengthening muscles that need to be conditioned or reconditioned. The children also connect with the animals emotionally, which seems to facilitate rehabilitation. After the therapy sessions, I went horseback riding with some of the staff. I am not a horse person. I like horses; I just don't necessarily like to ride them. When I was invited to ride for the first time with some of the other volunteers, I was a bit apprehensive. Janine and Lee, two of the volunteers, are a breed of lady that I affectionately call "horsewomen." A horsewoman would more readily give up her husband than her horse.

When Janine, in her thick Cockney accent, asked, "Patrick, would you care to take a ride?" I eagerly agreed although I was a little nervous. We went to the stables to pick out the horse that was to be my mount. There were a couple of options—Candice, an aged mare who was more interested in munching grass than hauling my six-foot-four frame around the woods, and Koda, a fiery half Arabian that hoofed the ground and threw his head around as if to ask, "You want a piece of me?"

Janine asked me if I had any experience with horses, and my bravado took over, and I said indignantly, "Of course I have experience with horses. Who do you think you're talking to?"

To be honest, the only horseback riding experience I had was at summer camp and a tandem ride with my mom's cousin Sandy in Texas when I was nine years old, but I told Janine that Koda was to be my horse for the day, and I confidently guided him out of the barn. Janine took Candice. Sitting on top of Koda, I had the confidence of John Wayne. If Koda pulled right, I pulled left. If he acted like he wanted to lunge forward, I jerked back on the reins with a hearty "whoa, boy." We began our walk down the trail, and I was lulled into a sense of security amplified by the cool breeze and gentle rocking motion of my trusted steed. As we rounded a bend in the trail, we entered into a straightaway through the woods.

Lee asked me, "Do you want to run him?"

If rational thought and cockiness were in a foot race, cockiness would have won on that day because, before I knew it, I said, "I'll see you at the finish line," and took off. In the movies, if a cowboy wants his horse to run he kicks him in the ribs with both heels. In the real world, if you want an Arabian to run, you gently squeeze your legs against his sides. I watch too many movies. I kicked Koda twice in the ribs, and all I heard was a grunt, which in horse talk means, "Oh no, you didn't." Before I knew it, Lee and Janine were racing down the trail, and Koda was bucking and crow hopping, trying to send me flying. This was not camp. I was in the middle of the woods, five miles from nowhere, strapped to a thousand pounds of whoop ass, holding on with every bit of strength I could muster. As Koda jumped and bucked, the saddle I was seated in started to slip to the side. Now if there was one place I wanted to be less than on top of an angry bucking bronco, it was underneath an angry bucking bronco. I had to get off. I made the decision to jump and was looking for the right moment when it happened. The saddle suddenly righted itself, and I was back on top. I went from being a terrified, whimpering little boy with my mind screaming, "Get off, get off, get off!," to instantly transforming back into John Wayne, yelling, "Ride, cowboy, ride!" I can't recall the exact moment my butt left the saddle. I just remember one moment thinking, "I can do this," and the next moment seeing blue sky and black boots. If you want to know what if feels like to be thrown from a horse, stand up on your bed, jump as high as you can in the air, and land on the floor, flat on your back. As I lay trying to recapture my lost breath among the sticks and leaves and mud, I saw Koda running down the trail. He looked back at me a couple of times, and I don't care what the experts say about horse psychology ... he was smiling. I lay on the ground, trying to catch my breath and determine if I had any broken bones, when Janine and Lee rode up. Janine had Koda's reins in hand and passed them to me. I looked at this animal that had sent me airborne and remembered something my grandfather used to tell me. My grandfather was a tough man, a quiet man, a Texan. He would say, "Son, if you ever get thrown from a horse, get right back on." That old man was crazy. I came up with a new philosophy on that day. Sometimes when you get thrown off of your horse, it is best to find a new horse.

Do you know someone that has been or have you ever been confronted with the same problem or problematic individual, and instead of finding resolution or common ground, you have the same argument or end up in the same position of nonproductivity? Sometimes instead of fighting the same fight over and over again in the same way, it is best to change tactics or change horses. Although it is crucial to always remain in alignment with your purpose statement and values, it is equally as critical to be willing to adapt new tools or methods of doing the same business and solving problems.

When I married my wife a few years ago, I moved to Burlington, North Carolina. We thought it would be better for me to move from Nashville instead of uprooting my stepson, Jack, from his family in the area. Besides, my in-laws were not going to let their grandson go without a fight, and I think my mother-in-law would fight dirty. I acclimated well to Burlington, especially after a monumental event that happened a few of years ago that forever changed the landscape of the small town North Carolina town— we got a Starbucks. I know that it is hard to imagine life without Starbucks, but not that many years ago, it was still a relatively new addition to small-town America. Although I lived in Nashville for a number of years prior to moving to North Carolina, I had successfully managed to steer clear of four-dollar coffee. My younger brother, Brent, lives in Charlotte, where he makes a lot of money in medical sales. I could do okay living in Charlotte. I have lived in big towns before, but my brother could not make it in Burlington, and he would give you two reasons why: no P. F. Chang's, and until recently, no Starbucks. Imagine my excitement when I was reading the Saturday morning newspaper and saw the headline as bright as day— STARBUCKS COMES TO ALAMANCE COUNTY.

I was so excited that I called my brother and said, "Hey, Bubba, guess what? We're getting a Starbucks."

He started to laugh on the other end of the line. He then said, "Son, you ain't ready for Starbucks."

"What do you mean I'm not ready for Starbucks?" I asked.

He said, "Patrick, you still buy your coffee from a gas station."

And he was right. But I could not wait to become a Starbucks coffee drinker. It was about time.

Imagine my excitement when, a couple of months later, I was driving through Burlington, North Carolina, and looked over where the old First State Bank building used to be, and there it was... "Grand Opening ... Starbucks." I was so excited that I pulled my minivan into the parking lot, got out, and ran to the front door. I opened the door and found a line that extended all the way to the back of the room. I jumped in line. I felt a little out of place, surrounded by intellectuals, college students, and professionals, because I was standing there in my blue jeans and ball cap. I knew my uncomfortable feeling would disappear, however, as soon as I became a Starbucks coffee drinker. As I approached the counter, I noticed the young lady taking orders. She was hard to miss. She had tattoos on her tattoos. She had earrings, nose rings, an eyebrow ring, and the piéce de résistance, a spike she had impaled through her tongue.

She looked up at me and said, "Walcum to Stwarbocks. May ah tak yo owrduh, pweese?"

I said, "Say what?"

"May ah tak yo owrduh, pweese?"

"Oh, my order. Of course you can take my order. I would like a cup of Starbucks coffee."

She then uttered the words that sent my world into a tailspin. She asked, "What kind?"

Have you ever gone into a new situation expecting grand results, only to have the exact opposite happen? This is what was happening to me. I had been so focused on the end result of a cup of Starbucks coffee that I had ignored the fact that in Starbucks, there is a process involved. I could feel the people in the line that had formed behind me growing impatient.

I looked at the young lady and said the only thing that came to mind, "Regular." Wrong answer.

She rolled her eyes and pointed to a menu board above her head. It was filled with Italian words. Words like "cappuccino," "espresso," "macchiato," "latte." To be honest with you, I had seen many of these words before but really didn't know what they meant or how they pertained to my coffee order.

I said, "I'll take a cappu ... How about a macchiat ... *Can't I just get a plain cup of coffee?*" She rolled her eyes once again and turned to a lonely urn on the counter behind her. She handed me a small cup of coffee, and I gave her a ten-dollar bill. She gave me my change. I paid $2.97 for that coffee, and to be honest with you, it tasted no better than the coffee I got at the BP station. I went back to my office, deflated. I had expected such big results and was disappointed that it was not turning out the way I had hoped. I decided to try again. The next morning at 7:00 a.m., I found myself at Starbucks, eagerly waiting in line. This time I prepared for my encounter with the tattooed lady by reading the menu board in advance.

When I approached the counter, the young lady said, "Walcum to Stwarbocks. May ah tak yo owrduh, pweese?"

I said, "Absolutely. Give me a capu ... cappuc ... *cappucino*." I was so proud. I felt like I finally fit into my surroundings. I had seen the Promised Land and walked right in. She then looked at me and uttered words that burst my self-confidence like a balloon.

She asked, "Tall, grande, or venti, skinny or regular, foam or no foam?"

I said, "Say what?" I know what "tall" is. I can figure out "grande" (we have a Taco Bell in Burlington), but "venti" had me stumped. I thought tall was tall. Not at Starbucks; at Starbucks, tall is short. I know what skinny is, and I have a couple of definitions for regular, although I had no idea what they had to do with coffee. As far as foam goes, I am a professional speaker, I have traveled all over this country, I have been to Myrtle Beach, and I've seen all kinds of foam. Never once have I considered putting it in my coffee—that's gross. I was back to square one. This was not working out the way it was supposed to. I shrugged my shoulders and said, "Just give me a plain cup of coffee." Another $2.97

later, I was back in my office, steaming mad, but I was not going to let this beat me. The best definition of insanity that I've heard is a man who tries the same thing over and over, expecting different results. I would not be that man. The next morning, I went back to Starbucks. This time instead of standing in line, I sat down, and I listened. I listened to the experienced coffee drinkers order—the college students, the professionals, and yes, the intellectuals. I made mental notes of their vocabulary and syntax, the meter and juxtaposition of phrasing. I created an order in my head that I felt bordered on poetry. I got in line but quickly discovered that I had been listening to the wrong people. I had been listening to people on diets, health enthusiasts, P90Xers! I got up to the counter and heard the familiar words again.

"Walcum to Stwarbocks. May ah tak yo owrduh, pweese?"

I said, "You bet. I would like a double-skinny, double-decaf latte, no fat, no whip, no foam."

She asked, "You want soy?"

"No soy."

"Anything else?" she asked.

"Oh yeah. I would like that in a tall cup with a short straw, make it extra hot, and give me one of those cute little cardboard cup holders so I don't burn my fingers."

She said, "Is that all?"

"Miss, I'm just getting started. In addition to my double-skinny, double-decaf latte, no fat, no whip, no foam, no soy, tall cup, short straw, extra hot with cute little cardboard cup holder, I would like a … I need a … I just got to have a … *biscotti*."

She gave me a cup of hot skim milk and a cookie that tasted like a doggie biscuit. She charged me $7.35. My brother was right. I wasn't ready for Starbucks, but imagine my excitement when I read in the Burlington newspaper that we were getting a Hooters.

I am proud to say that I am now an expert Starbucks coffee orderer, only because time, experience, and observation has made me so. What was once a cause for fear and trepidation has now become second nature. What about you? Are you staring at change? Maybe it's a new position, relationship, or compliance initiative being implemented. As frustrating and intimidating as it is to deviate from the status quo, true growth happens within the margin of uncertainty. The artists who enjoy longevity in the music business are willing to evolve throughout their careers. The willingness to embrace and leverage change is the difference between downloading fifty-year-old artists off of iTunes and having to find them by thumbing through vinyl at a vintage record store.

Exceed

The man who does more than he is paid for will soon be paid for more than he does.

—Napoleon Hill

Whole-Grain Pancakes

1 cup whole-wheat flour
½ cup rolled oats
¼ cup cornmeal
3 tablespoons flaxseed meal
3 tablespoons sugar
1 teaspoon baking powder
½ teaspoon baking soda
1 egg
2 cups buttermilk
Pam

Stir together the whole-wheat flour, oats, cornmeal, flaxseed meal, baking powder, brown sugar, and baking soda.
Pour in buttermilk and egg.
Stir until smooth.
Heat large skillet over medium heat.
Coat with cooking spray.
Pour 1/3 cup of batter onto skillet, and cook until bubbles form and the edges are dry.
Flip and cook until other side is browned.

If you had been standing next to me on any particular Saturday in the early to mideighties, you would have seen me toiling behind a twenty-one-inch Snapper push lawn mower. It was when I was twelve years old that I discovered that money doesn't grow on trees, but it does grow in yards. I was the sweaty, grime-covered neighborhood kid who mowed almost every yard on our block. Back then, we didn't have those big residential landscaping companies that nip, tuck, and liposuck your yards. You had me, a prepubescent penny pincher trying to earn extra money for the arcade. I charged ten dollars for a small yard and fifteen dollars for a big one, and Judge Nix had the biggest yard in our neighborhood. Had I known that it would take almost six hours to mow, I probably would have charged more than fifteen dollars, but that was the deal we agreed on. Every other Saturday, spring through fall, I mowed the judge's yard. One Saturday afternoon, I had been mowing all day long. I was hot, tired, and ready to go home. When I finished the last row, I cut the mower off and began to push it across the yard to the curb where my dad was going to pick me up. As I pushed the mower, I glanced over my shoulder and noticed the row of shrubs on the far side of the yard. Judge Nix had planted them the previous spring, and I had forgotten that behind them laid a strip of grass about four feet wide and twelve feet long that I had forgotten to mow. As I considered my mistake, I decided that I was too tired, too hot, and too ready to go home to finish the job, and since you couldn't see it from the street, it was no big deal. I continued to push the mower to the curb, and my conscience began to speak to me, telling me that I needed to finish mowing the yard. I began to rationalize that no one would notice it, and since part of it was in the neighbor's yard, it didn't matter. I finally sat on the curb, and Judge Nix came out and handed me a check for fifteen dollars. When my dad arrived, I helped him get the mower in the back of the truck, and then he began to walk around the yard, inspecting my work. As he walked toward the shrubs, I began to realize that, even though you couldn't see the unmowed grass from the street, he was about to discover it. He saw that I had not finished my work and gave me the "come here" gesture with his forefinger.

I reached my dad, and he said, "Son, you're not finished."

I said, "Daddy, I'm tired."

He said, "Son, you're not finished."

"Daddy, no one's going to notice it."

Finally in exasperation, my dad said, "Son, what do I always tell you? Don't ever do a job you're not willing to sign your name to. Are you willing to sign your name to this job?"

"Yes, sir."

My dad and I walked back across the yard in silence. Dad pulled the mower out of the truck and pushed it across the yard. He started it up and cut the grass behind the shrubs. It took him all of forty seconds. When he got back over to me, he asked if the judge had paid me.

"Yes, sir. Fifteen dollars."

My dad then looked me in the eye and said, "Give it back."

I said, "Say what?"

"Give it back," he repeated.

I was stunned.

He said, "Son, you don't want to get paid for incomplete work."

I said, "Yes, I do."

He said, "Then you shouldn't want to get paid for incomplete work."

I had been mowing that yard for almost seven hours in the Alabama heat and humidity, and now I had to give back the check. I wouldn't speak to him for a week.

Fast-forward twenty-five years. My wife and I purchased a new house and had some remodeling to do. We knocked out a wall to open up space, ripped up the carpet, put down hardwood floors, and painted the whole house. Painting is the one thing that my wife lets me do, and I quickly discovered why they call it faux finish. When you are married to a perfectionist like I am, you will paint it "fo'" times "'fo'" you are finished.

One Saturday afternoon, I had been painting all day long. I was hot, tired, and ready to quit. I had just finished the half bath downstairs, put my paints away, and come back in to inspect my work. After a day of stripping wallpaper, sanding, priming, and painting, I was ready for some relaxation. As I looked around the small bathroom, I noticed a spot behind the toilet that I had missed. It was only noticeable if you bent over, craned your neck, and looked at the five-inch-by-five-inch spot on the wall. I thought to myself, "Nobody is going to notice." I then remembered the lesson my father taught me almost twenty-five years earlier. We have all heard the phrase "Go the extra mile." The extra mile is easy to identify. It is not always easy to do, but it is easy to see. My dad was teaching me that true success and distinction is not measured in miles but rather in inches. It is the little bit extra that we give, the little extra we do, even when we think no one is looking, that creates loyal customers, teammates, or employees. It also creates distinction and makes us stand out among the competition.

You are an inch away from extraordinary. As I write this, the 2012 Olympic Games are happening in London, and my eleven-year-old son is enthralled. I am a bit surprised and pleased at his enthusiasm, especially since he is not typically interested in sports. He is active in the Boy Scouts and working toward a black belt in tae kwon do, but traditional sports like soccer and baseball have never held his interest. He is glued to the television, spouting statistics and obscure athletes' names, which leads me to believe that I may not have a star athlete on my hands, but I just might have one hell of a bookie. As we watch the swimming competition, I am struck by the slim margins that exist between a gold medal and last place. Mere one-hundredths of a second frame the divide between immortalization and obscurity. Years of grueling work, discipline, and exertion are ratified by fractions of an inch. The same margins of excellence frame your brand as well. Whether you are in sales, customer service, education, or management, the smallest deviation from the status quo can create the perception of what is extraordinary and what is merely mediocre. We are defined by the way we exceed expectations but also by the way fail to meet expectations. I wrote the following poem as a reminder of how perception defines a brand and how fragile that brand can be.

The Tortellini and the Hair

If you could have but one last meal
What would that banquet be
A common fare of potatoes and steak
Or splendiferous delicacies

Now I'm just a simple man
Whose roots crisscross the South
Dip it, dunk it, fry it twice
That's music to my mouth

Let me tell you a story about a man
Whose choice would be quite clear
His passion to partake of pasta plates
Tortellini's what he held most dear

The man's name was Ebenezer
But alas he was no scrooge
Simply a man who embraced
The singular taste of pasta in *rag'u*

He'd loved those belly button noodles
Ever since he was a child
Heaping bowls piled high to the sky
Would drive his taste buds wild

Most kids his age were eating PB and J
Grilled cheese, or hot dog weenies
But not the child with the sauce covered smile
His pick was tortellini

Tortellini in sauce, ragu, or broth
He loved them equally
Oodles and oodles of cheese-filled noodles
Was all he yearned to eat

Over time, the pull of the pasta grew stronger
He found himself on a crusade
A lifelong quest for the unparalleled best
Tortellini ever made

He dined at bistros, cafés, restaurants, and chains
In search of the elusive dish
But his attitude soured with each bite he devoured
For none matched his perfect wish

He could not rest till he found the best
He searched for the perfect plate
With each capacious feast, his girth increased
In response to the carbs that he ate

"Tortellini ,tortellini, tortellini," he muttered
Over and over again
His sanity and his Sansabelt slacks
Were both stretched remarkably thin

When one day on a bus, an old man heard his fuss
"This tortellini of which you speak
If you search for the best, let me put you to rest
For I have the answer you seek.

Why, I've had the world's best tortellini
Forty years ago last May
The sauce was of cream, the texture a dream
I can taste it to this very day."

Ebenezer sat up, his eyes all afire
"Tell me, sir, where was it cooked
For I must have a plate before it's too late
Only a few places I haven't looked."

The old man told of a trip through Bologna
A city in north Italy
For it was there that he dined on prosciutto and wine
And the world's best tortellini

Ebenezer begged for directions
Then bought a ticket on Alitalia Air
The holy grail within grasp finally at last
His quest for the best would end there

He wandered the streets of Bologna
Searching for the grand eatery
Praying it still existed among the so many listed
Then all at once, behold, there it be!

He walked in and sat down at a table
The cloth was of red, white, and greenie
The waiter, he said, *"Buona sera"*
Ebenezer said, "Tortellini!"

"Ahhhh, very good choice," said the waiter
"The chef's speciality."
Ebenezer took a sip of chianti
And said, "Bring on the tortellini!"

The *ristorante* met all expectations
The waiter was full of charm
The violinist played lovely sonatas
The ambiance inviting and warm

Then came the world's best tortellini
The *ristorante* erupted in cheers
He said this recipe's been in
Chef's family for well over five hundred years

Ebenezer was now rendered speechless
He could not believe his eyes
The tomatoes and cheese, garlic and cream
"This is it!" Ebenezer cried

He reached for his fork with determination
With reverence he took his first bite
His taste buds awakened , his hands stared shaking
His face could not hide his delight

He then took another bite of pasta
The next better than the rest
Oh, the sensation, the joyful elation
This tortellini was surely the best

As Ebenezer raised his fork in the air
Something strange caught his eye
In between the tongs, something did not belong
He was in for quite a surprise

A hair, a hair, it was a hair
What in the world was a hair doing there?
Suddenly, the pasta had lost all its flair
Because of one single, lonely, rogue hair

His appetite began to vanish
He pushed the pasta away
He began to feel sick to his stomach
His face turning a greenish gray

The waiter, he begged for forgiveness
The chef tried to make amends
Though the pasta was great, sadly they were too late
He never ate tortellini again

Perhaps Ebenezer was a scrooge after all
Or maybe just eccentric or weird
But through the last verses a lesson emerges
A moral for all has appeared

Just like one drop of oil the bucket will spoil
One bad apple can ruin the lot
The smallest infraction can cause a reaction
That resounds like a fired cannon shot

Our achievements and past reputation
Can in an instant be suddenly gone
For we're not judged in the light of what goes right
But rather by what goes wrong

No matter how trifling the size of our task
The importance is left in the wake
For the smallest pebble carelessly flung
Can ripple across the whole lake

This is a story of cause and effect,
Not one of what's right or what's fair
So now here ends the sad parable
Of the tortellini and the hair

Every person within any organization shares the responsibility for the customer experience. From the CEO to the person who sweeps the floor, a remarkable customer experience is a collective effort. The collapse of the customer experience, however, often falls on the shoulders of the individual due to his or her actions or lack of actions.

Are you the tortellini? Or are you the hair?

What are the expectations people have of you? How can those expectations be exceeded?

Process

Plans are of little importance,
but planning is essential.

—Winston Churchill

Double-Coconut Pancakes

1½ cups all-purpose flour
2 tablespoons sugar
2 tablespoons flaked sweetened coconut
1 teaspoon baking powder
½ teaspoon salt
1 can light coconut milk (13½ ounce)
1 tablespoon melted butter
1 lightly beaten egg

Mix flour, sugar, coconut, baking powder, and salt in large bowl.
Mix coconut milk, butter, and egg. Stir well.
Combine wet and dry mixtures, and stir till smooth.
Pour ⅓ cup pancake batter onto medium-hot skillet.
When bubbles appear and edges are cooked, turn.
Cook another minute or so until done.

Have you ever had an urge to do something that didn't quite fit your personality or lifestyle? Maybe you decided to buy a motorcycle or get a tattoo. Maybe it was something at the other end of the spectrum like flower gardening or crochet. For me, it was a triathlon. I have always been somewhat of an athlete, although I was never that guy that newspaper reporters and cheerleaders followed around the football field or baseball diamond. I was into more nontraditional sports. I was a half-decent wrestler in high school. I ski bummed across Colorado and Utah one winter and have studied various martial arts. A couple of years ago, as forty was beginning to rear its ugly head on my horizon, I decided that I wanted to try something new. I had been doing mixed martial arts for almost ten years, mainly Brazilian jiujitsu and Muy Thai kickboxing. Every year that passed, the guys seemed to be getting younger and stronger, and they wanted to fight in a cage. I needed a new sport that allowed me to sweat but provided less opportunity to get punched and/or kicked in the face. Triathlon became my mission. My younger brother had competed in a few triathlons, and one Saturday afternoon over a couple of cold beers, he laid down the challenge. He said, "Why don't you try one?" I wasn't quite sure if I was triathlon material, but he then uttered the words that have been known to alter the course of history: "I dare you." That's all it took. I was on the computer, looking for the closest triathlon in my area and, lo and behold, there was one right in my backyard … three weeks later. I began a vigorous training regimen that would last for the next three weeks. I ran every day, I swam laps in the pool every day, and I borrowed a bike that I rode every day. A triathlon sprint is a half-mile swim, a sixteen-mile bike ride, and a 5 k run. By the time race day arrived, I was confident that I was ready.

I stood on the shore of Lake Cammack, surrounded by 499 other competitors, sizing up my competition, and I felt that my chances of success were better than average. I entered the water for the eight o' clock start time, and when the air horn sounded, a strange quiet filled my ears. I dove into the chaos like a porpoise. My whole world was reduced to stroke, stroke, breathe. Stroke, stroke, breathe. "I'm actually doing it." Stroke, stroke, breathe, stroke, stroke, breathe. "I can't believe I'm in a triathlon." Stroke, stroke, breathe, stroke, stroke, breathe. "I think I'm in the lead." Stroke, breathe, breathe. "Wow, this is getting tough." Stroke, breathe, breathe, breathe. "Man, I'm getting tired." Stroke, breathe, breathe, breathe, cough, breathe. "What in the hell have I gotten myself into?"

I was fifty yards into the race and on the verge of panic, thinking there was no way I was going to make it. My twenty-five-dollar goggles (that were guaranteed not to fog up) looked like a windshield in an ice storm. I was consuming lake water by the quart, and I was being passed by people who looked like they rolled straight off of the couch and into the lake. As I rounded the first buoy, I was passed by a woman in her sixties wearing a pink swim cap. Then, as if all of the irony in the universe came crashing down on my head, she kicked me right in the face. I began to think that cage fighting was safer. I dragged myself out of the lake and crawled onto my bike. I finished in grand style behind an eighth-grade girl who kept giving me the stink eye for what I assume was the grunting and moaning sounds that I was involuntarily making on mile eleven. The last leg of the race was the 5 k. Strength and endurance took me the first two miles, and the fear of humiliation of being beaten by a sixty-eight-year-old ass-kicking granny brought me home. I was a triathlete.

It wasn't very long into the race that I learned a life lesson that I happily share with you: *it takes longer than three weeks to train for a triathlon!*

A week later, I was speaking at a conference in New York and was having a drink in the lobby of the Marriott Marquis Hotel, talking to a man whom I had just met about my triathlon experience. I was actually bragging to this poor stranger, certain that he would be impressed with my athletic endeavors. He was very nice and congratulatory but then proceeded to tell me about the first time he competed in the Iron Man World Championship Triathlon in Hawaii. In case you don't know, the Iron Man is a 2.4-mile swim, a 114-mile bike ride, and a marathon. Had he put on a pink swim cap and kicked me in the face, I could not have been more shocked and deflated. As we talked about triathlons, he shared with me the training regimen that he had implemented in preparation for the Iron Man. It was not a three-week process but rather a yearlong system of training and diet that prepared him for the ultimate physical challenge. Only through systematic training can one successfully prepare for such an event. Scott McKain, in his book *All Business is Show Business*, discusses how generation X was raised on television. Big Bird, Bert and Ernie, and Captain Kangaroo were helping to teach us life lessons and arithmetic. *Schoolhouse Rock!* was teaching us what an adverb is and how a bill becomes a law. Scott talks about how my generation and especially younger generations not only expect entertainment to be a part of life's interactions but demand it. I believe that is why we are conditioned to want instant gratification. There is nothing fun or instantly gratifying about training for a year and a half for an event, but if we want to be great instead of good, it is the process that creates perfection. What do U2, Bon Jovi, and AC/DC have in common? Eighties rock bands? Yes, but they were also the highest-grossing tours of 2010. U2 and Bon Jovi were the top tours of 2011 only because AC/DC didn't tour. These are bands that have been around for over thirty years, and they are outselling Lady Gaga, Justin Bieber, and all of the other young artists making twelve-year-old girls shake with glee. Why? There are two reasons. One, they freakin' rock! They are not just good, they are great! After decades of experience, they have become masters of their craft, and it is reflected in their concert attendance. Two, they have been building their fan base for decades.

So often we focus on the results of greatness but not the process of getting there. "I want a six-figure income," "I want six-pack abs," or "I want to be famous." *American Idol* has, in my opinion, done a great disservice to America's youth. It has created the impression that true success can be achieved instantly when, in reality, true success is usually the result of years of committing to the process of getting good. My friend Gabe Martin is an amazing violin player and teacher. Gabe was telling me about his students who come to him wanting to be able to play beautiful pieces of Beethoven or Haydn. They want to be the next Itzhak Perlman or Michael Rabin. They are frustrated when their instruments squeak and squawk as they are learning the craft. Gabe patiently tells them to focus on the process of getting good. He says, "Focus on the scales and exercises, the theory, and hand position. Before you know it, the result of playing beautiful music has become a reality."

In order to achieve the final result of success—however we define it—we must first identity what our goals are. As the parent of young children, I am reminded of the words of my parents when I was a child in school. "Do well," "Study hard," "Hit the books." What does that mean? Those words meant nothing to me. So often we demand certain results of our children or our staff but don't outline a path to success. Peter Drucker coined the phrase "management by objectives." From management by objectives emerged SMART criteria which has been taught and discussed at length on various blogs and training systems as it pertains to project management and even personal development. SMART goals are specific, measurable, attainable, relevant, and time bound. To identify general goals without making them adhere to the SMART criteria is, in my opinion, setting yourself up for failure or distraction. In order for a team to be in tune, goals must first be identified and made SMART. Then a pathway to success or a process must be constructed and implemented. Focus on the process to achieve the results.

Most people make pancakes from memory. After a while, you learn the basic steps and then modify them to fit your style and tastes. It all starts, however, with a recipe—or a process. Focus initially on the process, and the result will be excellence.

COMPLIANCE

*The drummer's supposed to sit back there
and swing the band.*

—Buddy Rich

Chocolate Chip Pancakes

1½ cups all-purpose flour
3½ teaspoons baking powder
1 tablespoon sugar
3 tablespoons melted butter
1 egg
1¼ cups of milk
Mini chocolate chips
PAM cooking spray

Sift together flour, baking powder, salt, and sugar in a large
bowl.
Whisk in melted butter, egg, and milk until combined.
Let batter sit for 5 minutes.
Preheat a large pan over medium-high heat.
Spray with cooking spray.
Pour batter into the hot pan, about ⅓ cup of batter for each
pancake. Cook for 2–3 minutes, until bubbles appear on the
sides and center of each pancake.
Sprinkle mini chocolate chips on the uncooked side of each
pancake; continue cooking as usual.
Flip and cook until golden, about 1–2 minutes.

Compliance remains an expensive line item in many annual budgets. Whether you are talking about Sarbanes-Oxley, Dodd-Frank, or OSHA, failure to maintain compliance can be costly in fixed expenditures as well as liability. The compliance I am discussing in this chapter, however, is abstract. I am focusing on complying with existing protocols, proven methodology, or the experience of others. Did you learn how to make pancakes by reading the box or from watching your mother, grandmother, or dad do it? Anyone can read a recipe, but I learned to wait for the moment the bubbles start to appear before flipping the pancake from my mother. Sometimes you can arrive at your destination quicker by following a good leader. This is counterintuitive to much of what we've heard about leadership, but the best bandleaders know how and when to follow someone else's lead. Being able to follow, in my opinion, is probably the most important quality of good leaders. The best leaders know that in order to lead effectively, they must know when to be out front, and they need to know when to step back and let someone else take over. In a band, the most important person is not the lead singer but the drummer. If the singer stops singing, the crowd dances on. If the guitar player falls out, the crowd dances on. If the piano player, fiddler, or the horn section puts down their instruments, the crowd dances on, but if the drummer quits ... the crowd goes to the bar. The drummer is the glue that holds the band together. He sets the pace that the entire band plays to. Although usually not the lead singer, the drummer must be followed in order to have a cohesive team. For most organizations, the drummer is the team leader, project manager, or supervisor. The most effective leaders are the ones who set the tempo, step back, and let the band play.

In Nashville, you would be surprised at how many amazing musicians don't read music. If you were to go into a recording session, the charts that are used are not made up of bars of notes and rests but rather numbers, dots, and squiggles. This method of notation has come to be known as the Nashville number system. Classical musicians turn their noses up at the "Nashville cats" who are unable or more likely unwilling to use traditional scores of music, and Nashville musicians laugh at the classical musicians' inability to play what is not written down in front of them on a music stand. The number system is simple. It is a medium for improvisation that's basically a loose framework that shows the chord changes and various symbols representing accents or stops within the song. The songwriter or bandleader communicates to the band what style the song is to be played in, and the musicians improvise within the framework given. This method allows the musicians to experiment and try what "feels right." Therefore, it is necessary for a musician to have a strong understanding of various styles of music. The Nashville number system allows bands to play songs without a lot of rehearsal. How many times have we had a manager or supervisor who micromanaged the team into a state nonproductivity? In order for a team to be in tune, you must first hire great people, then set the framework and the goals. Once those are in place, step back and let them jam. From my experience, the worst thing that a producer can do in the studio is to tell the musicians exactly what notes to play. An effective producer communicates vision, and the musicians offer their creativity within the context of their instruments.

When I was a business major in the 1990s, Total Quality Management (TQM) was ever present on the lips of every upper-level management student walking the Pine-Soled floors of Greene Hall at the University of Southern Mississippi. One prevailing concept that leapt out at me from the pages of Demming, Juran, and Crosby was their perception of the role that management should play when implementing TQM. Management was there to support the frontline employee, not the other way around. If there was a breakdown in productivity, the blame lay with the manager or process, not the worker on the line. Creating compliance is simply about shifting attitudes and perceptions. One of my favorite stories that I use to close many of my speeches is about a man and his grandson walking hand in hand down a busy sidewalk.

The little boy was mesmerized by the sights, sounds, and smells of the big city, so he stopped in his tracks when they came across a chain-link fence with a sign that said "Construction Site. Keep Out!" The little boy stood mesmerized with his face to the fence as he watched the activity on the other side. His attention turned to an old man mixing mortar. The old brick mason put some mortar on a brick with his trowel and then placed bricks on the foundation. He repeated the process and then stacked the bricks on top of the other.

"What's that man doing?" asked the little boy.

The grandfather said, "That man is a brick mason.

He is building a wall." Overhearing the conversation, the mason walked over to the fence and spoke directly to the child, saying, "I'm not building a wall; I'm building a beautiful cathedral."

The brick mason defined his job not by the task he performed but rather by the outcome produced. A bad manager or team leader will micromanage the team into a state of nonproductivity. When our role is defined by outcomes, we have pride in our work, satisfaction in our jobs, and camaraderie among our teams. Compliance is the ability to not only adhere to rules and tasks but to work within the framework that supports the vision. A good leader will communicate that vision and support the role of the individual in creating the vision.

Ask yourself, what outcomes am I seeking to produce? What do I need to do to make those outcomes a reality? What has been done in the past that produced the outcomes I desire?

INCLUSION

You want to go where everybody knows your name.

—Theme from *Cheers*

Pineapple Upside-Down Pancakes

Prepare batter according to Old-Fashioned Pancake recipe.

Drain a can of pineapple rings.
Save some of the liquid to replace the liquid in recipe.
Set a pineapple ring on the heated skillet.
Place a maraschino cherry in center of ring.
Ladle approximately $\frac{1}{4}$ cup of batter onto the ring.
Cook as directed.

The sense of belonging is one of the most basic human needs. If you took an introductory psychology class in college, you learned about behavioral psychologist Abraham Maslow's hierarchy of needs pyramid. In Maslow's 1943 paper, *A Theory of Human Motivation*, he identified the five areas of human needs. The first level covered physiological needs, such as breathing, food, water, and sex. (It's a need. It's science. Guys win.) These needs must be satisfied before you can progress to the next level. The next level involves safety needs, such as shelter, job security, not being eaten by a bear. Then comes love and belonging, followed by self-esteem needs and self-actualization. The need for belonging is a powerful influence for healthy and profitable relationships, whether they are with the customer, coworkers, or teams or within your community.

Not long after I moved to Nashville in the mid-nineties, I met a group of guys that I started hitting the town with. Back in those days, I had a flat stomach, a tolerance for Jack Daniel's, and a tendency to see dawn as the end of an evening. Now my six-pack has turned into a one-pack, the smell of Jack Daniel's makes me queasy, and dawn is often the backdrop for my second cup of coffee. We were all aspiring artists, musicians, songwriters, or studio engineers, which meant we were broke. One guy in our group worked for RCA Records … in the mail room. I used to wonder what an intelligent, college-educated, ambitious guy like him was doing working for nine bucks an hour in the mail room of a record label. I finally understood one night when we all went to a downtown Nashville nightclub.

At RCA, all of the employees received an RCA jacket. They looked like high school letterman jackets with the RCA logo on the back. When we walked into the club that night and people saw his jacket, you would have thought royalty had entered the room. Keep in mind that 80 percent of the people in the bar were trying to make it in the music business, and as far as they were concerned, he could make their dreams come true. Beautiful women were brushing past me to brush against my friend. Guys were buying him drinks, and bartenders were passing him their demos. I then understood why a college-educated, intelligent, ambitious guy would work in the RCA mail room for nine bucks an hour. He wasn't working for nine bucks an hour. He was working for the jacket. RCA had created a sense of belonging among their employees that encompassed everyone from the C suite to the mail room. They were a part of something bigger than themselves, and it created an atmosphere of inclusion that translated into a job satisfaction that was not predicated by salary. People want to do business with people who enjoy their jobs. They are happier, friendlier, more helpful, and nicer. When a culture of belonging exists, people will work harder, be more content, and perform at a higher level.

When I ran a kickboxing gym, I discovered how value could be created that had nothing to do with money. I'm not much of a kickboxer, but I enjoy mixed martial arts, so when I was asked to take over a Nashville Muy Thai kickboxing gym, I agreed. I needed to hire great instructors, and since the gym wasn't bringing in a lot of money at first, I couldn't pay them a lot. I ended up paying them fifteen dollars for each class they taught, and they were lining up to teach. Why would someone want to work for fifteen dollars? I knew I had to motivate them with something other than money. It turned out that the cardio kickboxing class was a huge hit among women. We promoted the heck out of it, and after a while, it was filled with beautiful women. Needless to say, the guys were dying to teach those classes. I put their pictures on a poster with their fight stats and displayed them prominently on the wall, which created (local) celebrity status. We continued to promote their brand, which enabled them to make money off of private lessons. They drew value from being a part of the gym that had nothing to do with the fifteen dollars they got for teaching a class. Study after study reveals that money is much lower on the list of job-satisfaction triggers than things like "I like the people I work with," "My opinion is valued," or "I feel like I am serving the greater good." By creating a culture of belonging, you will increase productivity and profitability.

ACCOUNTABILITY

No snowflake in an avalanche ever feels responsible.

—Voltaire

Sour Cream Pancakes

2 tablespoons butter
1 cup flour
2 tablespoons sugar
$\frac{1}{2}$ teaspoon baking soda
1 teaspoon baking powder
$\frac{1}{2}$ teaspoon salt
2 eggs, slightly beaten
1 cup sour cream
$\frac{1}{4}$ cup milk

Melt butter and cool.
Beat together eggs and sour cream.
Add cooled butter and milk.
Mix dry ingredients together.
Stir in liquid mixture until well blended.
Pour $\frac{1}{3}$ cup of batter onto medium skillet.
Wait until bubbles form on surface, and then flip.
Cook for 1 more minute until golden brown.

Former AT&T CEO Michael Armstrong is famously quoted as saying, "The ancient Romans had a tradition. Whenever one of their engineers constructed an arch, as the capstone was hoisted into place, the engineer assumed accountability in the most profound way possible: he stood underneath the arch."

I was recently at an event in Charlotte where I had the chance to meet an interesting man named Oliver Moore III, who had made his career working in the cutthroat world of New York newspaper and magazine publishing. We were talking about the slow, bleeding death of hard-copy magazines, and I told him that before she gave it up, they would have to pry *Us Weekly* magazine out of my wife's cold, dead fingers. He smiled and told me that he was the original editor of *Us Weekly*. I had no idea I had been in the presence of celebrity gossip royalty. I couldn't wait to tell my wife. We talked about journalism and the impact that blogs, social media, and wireless devices have had on the dissemination of news and the public perception. The good news is that, thanks to Twitter, YouTube, and Facebook, we can receive information as it occurs. We followed the World Cup, the Arab Spring Revolution, presidential election results, and who the Kardashian girls are schtupping in real time. What can possibly be wrong with that? Accountability. He told me, "Patrick, as a journalist, I am bound by rules. Sources must be vetted, information must be validated, opinions are not fact, and Wikipedia is not a wellspring of truth. Bloggers, tweeters, and paparazzi are not bound by the same journalistic integrity that was instilled in me from the beginning of my career."

Without accountability, we are doomed to versions of the truth or outright falsehoods. There is a great line from the 1993 movie *Jurassic Park* where Jeff Goldblum's character, Dr. Ian Malcolm, is confronting billionaire John Hammond. He said, "I'll tell you the problem with the scientific power that you're using here. It didn't acquire any discipline to attain it. You read what others have done, and you took the next step. You didn't earn the knowledge for yourself, so therefore, you don't take any responsibility for it."

If you want to create an extraordinary customer, employee, or coworker experience, you will need two things: liking and trust. If your customers, teammates, or employees don't feel that you are accountable for your actions and responsible for the outcomes you produce, then there can be no trust.

A few years ago, my lawn man died. It took me by surprise when my mother-in-law showed me the obituary, but there it was in black and white … Dennis was gone. Dennis was a really nice man, and although I didn't know him very well, we did have a couple of meaningful conversations, leaning against the fence that separates my property from my next-door neighbor's. As a boy in Auburn, Alabama, I painstakingly mowed almost every yard in the Bent Creek subdivision. I used to fantasize about one day having a lawn man to do it for me. Now I did—and now he was gone. I miss him, but I faced a dilemma. Dennis charged the same rate for twenty-five years. Even when gas spiked at almost four dollars a gallon, Dennis held firm. His rate was far below what the big landscaping companies in our area charged—and there was no way I was going to pay that—so I decided to man up and get back into the business of mowing lawns ... my lawn. After a testosterone-filled trip to Lowe's (full of grunting, pointing, and kicking the tires of the zero-turn-radius lawn mowers), I arrived home with a new push mower, a weed eater, and a high-powered blower. I was locked, cocked, and ready to rock. I now mow my own lawn and have discovered a few truths that I feel are worth sharing. First of all, I love mowing my yard. I feel a sense of pride and satisfaction when I am finished that I never did as a kid. This came as quite a surprise to me because, for years, the smell of fresh-cut grass reminded me of hours of hard labor in the unforgiving Alabama sun. Secondly, I discovered that I do a better job than Dennis did. Don't misunderstand me; I am not disparaging Dennis in any way, but I wasn't paying him enough to pick up sticks, trim shrubs, and edge the driveway. He came once a week, mowed, and left. Finally, I now know every inch of my property. This sounds a bit silly, especially since I have lived in my house for years, but when you are responsible for managing your own yard, you become familiar with every nook, cranny, root, rut, and problem area.

So why now? Why do I now feel differently about doing something I despised as a kid? One word: accountability. I own my property; therefore, I am accountable for its appearance. I own my property; therefore, I am accountable for its functionality and purpose. If I don't manage a routine maintenance schedule, the blame for the appearance of my yard lies with me. Why? Because I own it, and I am accountable. So how do *you* create accountability? You may not sign your own paycheck, but when you claim responsibility for the outcome of your organization, team, customers, clients, product lines, territories, or personal life, you begin to control the outcome. It's the perception of ownership that creates responsibility. Responsibility creates accountability, and accountability leads to empowerment. When you are empowered, you begin to influence outcomes.

Three Paths to Accountability

1. **Get your hands dirty.** I once spoke for a restaurant chain that required all of the management trainees to sweep the parking lot for a week. I was told that at the end of the week, the trainees would be able to fully understand and appreciate the job they were asking restaurant employees to do—as well as know *exactly* how long it should take to complete the task.

2. **Intimately know your (yard, product, service).** My friend Jimmy Prophet sells industrial batteries. He not only knows his product, he knows so much about the equipment that utilizes his product that company engineers call him in to solve problems they can't. Do you think his competition can intimidate him by undercutting his price? *No way.* He is a valuable resource.

3. **Maintain your (mower).** It is amazing how much easier it is to cut my grass when I have the blade sharpened regularly. Is your company too cheap to buy you a new laptop? Buy

your own. Boss too stingy to reimburse for client meals? If it closes the deal, pay for it yourself. You are the owner. It's time to stop complaining and cut the grass.

TIMING

Luck is what happens when preparation meets opportunity.

—Seneca

Blueberry Pancakes

$1\frac{1}{2}$ cups all-purpose flour
$3\frac{1}{2}$ teaspoons baking powder
1 tablespoon sugar
3 tablespoons melted butter
1 egg
1 cup frozen blueberries
$1\frac{1}{4}$ cups of milk
PAM cooking spray

Sift together flour, baking powder, salt,
and sugar in a large bowl.
Whisk in melted butter, egg, and milk until combined.
Gently stir in 1 cup of frozen blueberries.
Let batter sit for 5 minutes.
Preheat a large pan over medium-high heat.
Spray with cooking spray.
Pour batter into the hot pan, about $\frac{1}{3}$ cup of batter for each
pancake. Cook for 2–3 minutes, until bubbles appear on the
sides and center of each pancake.
Flip and cook until golden, about 1–2 minutes.

T ed Williams—the name of a man beloved by generations of Americans throughout the decades. A name that conjures up memories of ballparks, home runs, and heroic slides into home plate. Over the years, the name Ted Williams has become synonymous with excellence in baseball ... until now. Another Ted Williams emerged and grabbed America by the heartstrings, bringing new meaning to the name. It is no longer just synonymous with baseball but also with redemption and second chances.

We all heard the story. A homeless man panhandling on a dreary off ramp in Columbus, Ohio, holds a sign that simply says, "I have a God-given voice. I'm an ex–radio announcer who has fallen on hard times ... Please help." A local news reporter finds it interesting so he asks him to "work for his dollar." Thanks to a video camera, YouTube, and the law of exponential growth, Ted Williams went from a homeless man to a household name in a matter of days. He has had appearances on the *Today Show* and radio interviews and has received employment offers from around the country. It is a true rags-to-riches story, and what a story it is. Drugs and alcohol steal the future of a promising radio announcer, only for him to be given a second chance. It's like winning the lottery ... or is it? I keep hearing the comparison between Ted Williams's story and winning the lottery, and I can't disagree more. I am not blind to the fortuitous circumstances that led to his newfound fame, but what is being overlooked in the media is the fact that Ted Williams, despite his faults, was ready! Let's look at the facts.

1. Ted Williams has natural ability. His voice is deep and rich.
2. He went to school to develop his natural voice into a "voice for radio."
3. He is no stranger to the control room. He knows the equipment and the process.
4. Ted Williams had his pitch down cold: "When you're listening to nothing but the oldies, you're listening to Magic 98.9."

When the reporter said, "I'm going to make you work for your dollar," Ted Williams didn't stutter, stammer, or back away. He jumped at the chance to perform what he has so obviously been practicing for years. When the opportunity came, Ted Williams grabbed it and became an overnight sensation twenty-five years in the making. What about you? Do you believe in luck? Or do you believe that you create your own? The Roman philosopher Seneca said, "Luck is what happens when preparation meets opportunity." Does Ted Williams find himself in his current circumstance because he has a deep voice? No. Many people have deep voices. It is the combination of raw talent, developed talent, and good old-fashioned timing.

I had been living in Nashville for a couple of years when I bought some new recording equipment. This was before Pro Tools, Cakewalk, and other recording software emerged, making it possible for thirteen-year-old aspiring artists to produce radio-quality albums in their bedrooms. It was a simple eight-track recording device that I was going to use to record guitar- vocals. I was so impressed that I could create my own demos that I overlooked the simple fact that the quality sucked, and this came back to bite me in a big way. I returned to Nashville one afternoon after playing a weekend of shows in Columbus, Ohio. I lived on White Bridge Road across from Nashville Tech and less than a mile up the road was a Subway franchise. I decided to grab a sandwich on the way into town, and when I returned to my truck, I found the battery dead. Perfect! I stood there staring under the hood, trying to will it back to life, when a guy walked out and asked if I needed a hand. I told him that I would appreciate a lift to my house, so I grabbed my guitar and got in his car. Seeing that I was a musician, he began asking questions, and I started to get the impression that he was in the music business. I told myself to play it cool. We got to my house, and he handed me his card and told me that he would like to hear a demo.

"You're in the business?" I asked.

He smiled and said, "Drop your tape off at the office."

I never even looked at his card as I shook his hand and got out. Standing in my living room, I slowly turned the card over like a kid on Christmas morning and the words "Frank Liddell, Head of A&R, Decca Records" jumped out at me. I was stunned. What were the odds that the one guy at a major record label with the power to sign new acts was in my driveway, asking for a demo? I spent the rest of the evening thanking my lucky stars for a dead battery and recording songs into my eight-track recorder. I layered the guitars, added harmony, and stopped periodically to pat myself on the back for recording my own demo. It never even crossed my mind that I might be better off paying a professional to produce my demo. The next morning, I dropped the tape off at Decca Records, and the receptionist even told me that Mr. Liddell was expecting it. I went home and waited for my phone to ring. It never did. Everything had lined up for me that day—a chance meeting with an A&R director for a major record label, the fact that I apparently intrigued him enough to want to hear my songs, and perfect timing in the fact that label was looking for new acts. What was not going for me that day was the one thing that I had absolute control over: preparation. I was not ready for the opportunity. I'm sure that he put the tape in the player, listened to thirty seconds of the home-made demo, said, "This sucks," and promptly forgot about me. Had this happened a few years later after I was a bit more seasoned as an artist and with better quality representations of my work, it may have had a much different result.

It is my firm belief that most young singers who move to Nashville to make it as recording artists have a chance to be heard. Most are not ready for the opportunity when it comes. Whether you are in sports, the arts, sales, education, or any myriad of professions, defining moments appear regularly. Most are not prepared to grasp the opportunity. Preparation is the only way to create perfect timing. Are you ready for the opportunities when they come your way?

Four Ways to Become An Overnight Success

1. **Excellence in what you do.** According to Malcolm Gladwell's *Outliers*, mastery is achieved after ten thousand hours of practice. When

you practice every day, grabbing the defining moments becomes second nature.

2. `Focused expertise. The more specific you can be in defining what you do, the easier it is to find a fit. Ted Williams didn't have a sign that said, "I have a great voice; put me to work." He said he could do voice-over work, thus making it easy to identify his value.

3. Affability. People want to do business with those whom they like and trust. Ted Williams is a humble, likeable guy. If he had been arrogant, smug, or ornery, the response would have been negligible. Be nice.

4. Supporting materials. Have quality head shots or photos taken every three or four years. You don't have to be in the public eye to have a need for quality pictures. You never know when you will make the news or have a client or event where a good picture is needed. It makes you look professional, and you control the way the world sees you.

PRESENCE

Forever is composed of nows.

—Emily Dickinson

Buttermilk Pancakes

1½ cup all-purpose flour
2 teaspoons white sugar
¼ teaspoon salt
½ teaspoon baking powder
¼ teaspoon baking soda
¾ cup buttermilk
¼ cup milk
1 egg
2 tablespoons butter
1 teaspoon vanilla

Heat pan to medium heat.
Mix together dry ingredients in a bowl.
In another bowl, whisk together milk, egg, butter, and vanilla.
Combine both dry and wet mixtures.
Pour ⅓ cups of batter onto pan.
When tops begin to bubble after a couple of minutes, flip.
Cook another minute until golden.

I'll never forget calling my dad after a long day of waiting tables and telling him that I'd had it. I was through with putting up with rude customers, demanding managers, and a particularly ornery dishwasher, just to barely earn enough money to scrape by. I told him that this wasn't what I went to college for, and I was thinking about giving up on the music business and getting a "real job." I waited for the sigh of relief that I was sure he had been holding in since I first broke the news that I was Nashville bound, but it didn't come. Instead, he told me something that admonished me, inspired me, and added the touch of perspective that I needed. He said, "Son, bloom where you're planted." He told me that I would not be a waiter forever, but if I couldn't be excellent at something as simple as serving food, how was I going to create excellence in other areas of my life? He was simply telling me to be present. A lightbulb turned on in me, and I decided that even though I didn't particularly enjoy the task at hand, it didn't mean I couldn't enjoy my job. I made the decision to bloom where I was planted and to be present. I changed my attitude, and I was friendlier to my customers, which created more income. I was friendlier to my coworkers, which created a fun work environment. Incidentally, some of my best friends today I met working in that restaurant, and many of the opportunities that I had in the music business were born there. My wife tells me (and whoever else is in the room) that I have BSO syndrome. Don't worry, it's not fatal, but it can be contagious. The "Bright Shiny Object syndrome" is a condition that affects certain right-brained people—like me—who allow themselves to become distracted from a task by refusing to fully commit to the job at hand. Many times, my wife has arrived home to find bushes partially trimmed, old wallpaper partially removed, or a half-made sandwich on the counter, only to find me in the backyard doing something else. She will simply ask, "Did something bright and shiny float past you?" A recent survey conducted by American Online and Salary.com shows that the average employee admits to wasting over two hours a day at work doing everything from surfing the web to socializing to applying for other jobs. Our inability to be present at work is not only costing us in productivity but costing employers over $750 billion a year in wasted salary.

Being present is not only critical in an office environment but also in our relationships. I was once told that "it's not the presents we give our children that count, but our presence with our children that counts." I only wish I had heard that advice before I spent all that money on iPods and Wii. Oftentimes, my eight-year-old, Robert will come up to me and say, "Daddy, I want to do something with you." He doesn't care if it's putt-putt, bowling, or kicking the soccer ball in the backyard. He just wants me to be present with him, and I am smart enough to know that he won't always feel that way. On the other hand, my stepson, Jack, has reached the point where he wants to be dropped off three blocks from the school to avoid being seen with the dorky dad in the minivan. Just like in our families, the best customer or coworker relationships are created when we are present.

Have you ever had a vendor, employer, or service provider make you feel unimportant by not being present? My wife and I recently had this experience when we refinanced our home. Over the last couple of years, I watched interest rates fall and held out until I felt they could go no lower before deciding to lock in. A few weeks prior to refinancing, I was giving a speech for a regional bank in North Carolina and was approached by the branch manager from my town. He introduced himself and told me the he would love to talk to me about how they could serve my banking needs. How could I say no? I would have thought something was wrong if he hadn't approached me, so I told him that I was planning to refinance my home and would stop by the office to discuss it. I met with him and his team and liked them so much that I decided to give them my business. When my loan was passed on to be administered by a third party was when things started to change. What started off as a friendly relationship with a local bank turned into a cold process with a third-party mortgage company. The only time my mortgage broker and I communicated was when I initiated contact. This left me feeling like I was driving this process, instead of the experienced professional. If you've ever bought or refinanced a home, you know that it can be a confusing, time-sensitive process where certain things have to happen in order. One day, I was particularly stressed out by a late appraisal report, so I called to inquire where we were in the process and was told, "Give me a second. I don't even know who you are." Talk about making me feel unimportant. Please don't misunderstand me. I am a reasonable person and understand that things go wrong and that I'm not his only client. I am, however, the only client who I care about! Unlike mortgage professionals, this process is not second nature to me, and when I feel disconnected, it causes stress.

According to an article written by John C. Groth in the *Journal of Product and Brand Management*, the Exclusive Value Principle attracts customers based on prestige and perceived value. Higher margins can be attained when a marketer identifies and fulfills psychic-based needs. An extraordinary customer experience is also created by emotion. Groth explains that when you appeal to the psychic needs of the customer, "the marketer can create premiums that do not exist." As humans, we all have a psychic need to feel special. When we make our customers feel important by being present, we create exclusive value that people will pay a premium for. I call this the Here and Now Principle. We create healthier and more profitable relationships when we are engaged in the moment and make the others feel special.

How to Be Present

1. **Communication.** Most people are reasonable and will understand when things go wrong. By creating strong lines of communication, you will create trust, which leads to healthier relationships and more profits. In 2001, the University of Michigan Health System created a claims management program that centered on full disclosure when dealing with medical errors instead of the "deny and defend" approach that exists at most hospitals. The new program proactively sought out medical errors and disclosed the found errors to

patients. When the provider was at fault, an explanation of the problem was given, and compensation was offered to the patient. According to a paper written by UMHS chief risk officer Rick Boothman, JD, and chief medical officer Darrell Campbell Jr., "there has been a 61% decrease in spending at the UMHS on legal defense costs which supports the possibility that patients may be less likely to file lawsuits when given transparency and an offer of compensation." By communicating more fully with patients, UMHS proved that they were present.

2.   **Management by objectives.** This is a process made popular in Peter Drucker's book *The Practice of Management.* MBO is a process that involves defining objectives within an organization so management and employees understand what needs to be done in order to achieve them. We so often get caught up in the stress that surrounds "work" that we either alienate those around us or we neglect the psychic-based needs of the customer. When we become task oriented, it is easier to prioritize and segment our day into manageable parts.

3.   **Attitude.** The attitude we choose impacts the way we are perceived both in the marketplace and in our relationships. When we choose to view our circumstances positively, we become more enjoyable to interact with. Jeffrey Gitomer states in *The Little Red Book of Selling,* "If

all things are equal, people want to do business with friends. If all things are not so equal, people STILL want to do business with their friends." Friendship is comprised of two key elements: liking and trust. The attitude you project will determine whether or not you are liked. Liking leads to better relationships, more productivity, and more profits.

CONSISTENCY

Success is neither magical nor mysterious.
Success is the natural consequence of consistently
applying the basic fundamentals.

—Jim Rohn

Red Velvet Pancakes

1 cup all-purpose flour
1 teaspoon baking powder
$1/4$ teaspoon baking soda
$1/4$ teaspoon salt
2 tablespoons sugar
2 tablespoons unsweetened cocoa powder
1 egg
$3/4$ cup buttermilk
$1/4$ cup sour cream
1 tablespoon red food coloring
1 teaspoon pure vanilla extract
3 tablespoons butter, melted

Whisk flour, baking powder, baking soda, salt, sugar, and
cocoa powder in a large bowl.
In another large bowl, beat egg with buttermilk, sour cream,
food coloring, and vanilla extract until smooth.
Slowly whisk in the flour mixture, adding melted butter in
gradually as well, until all lumps are out.
Heat a large nonstick pan over medium heat, and then drop
in batter $1/4$ cup at a time to form pancakes.
Flip when bottoms are set and bubbles are forming on top,
and cook until firm and fluffy all the way through.

Have you ever mixed pancake batter that was the wrong consistency? You have a hot mess on your hands. Too much water or milk, and the batter is runny; not enough, and you are making bricks. The consistency of the batter is as important to the success of making pancakes as the consistency of your brand is to the success of you or your organization.

As a student at the University of Southern Mississippi, I began a love affair that has endured throughout the better part of two decades. No, the affair of which I speak was not with one of the beautiful Southern belles that make up 60 percent of the student body but rather with a dirty, disgusting-looking, beady-eyed little creature called the crawfish. Until I ventured onto the USM campus in the early nineties, the only crawfish I had ever seen had been in the creek behind my parents' house, and the thought of actually putting it in my mouth never crossed my mind. Imagine my surprise and trepidation when I was invited to a fraternity party only to find rows of tables covered in newspaper, with piles of red, steaming crawfish waiting to be devoured. As the zydeco band played in the background, one of my buddies showed me how to pinch the head off of the little lobsterlike creature, peel back the first layer of shell on the tail, and pull the meat out with my teeth. I was hooked. It was the most wonderful-tasting food I had ever eaten. It even made the beer taste better. I later learned that for generations of Louisianans and southern Mississippians, crawfish is social fare in the same way that chili is for Texans, clams are for New Englanders, and fried catfish is for my native Alabamians. I also learned that they take pride in the spiciness of their crawfish. Cayenne pepper is the predominant seasoning for boiled crawfish, and for many daring souls, the hotter the better. When crawfish season was approaching, arguments would begin to float around the halls of the ATO house as my fraternity brothers would boast about who made the spiciest crawfish. When I later observed one of my drunken brethren writhing on the ground in pain, wiping his tongue after sampling a crawfish boiled in his personal blend of spice, I decided that it takes no great skill to dump heaps of cayenne pepper into a pot of boiling water. The real test is, can you eat your own crawfish?

Not long ago, I gave a speech for a major utility company in Tennessee. After the event, I was chatting with the meeting planner, who told me of a negative experience they had with a previous speaker. I was told that the speaker was really good, highly energetic, and well liked by the audience. She talked about not letting the little things get you down and negatively impact your attitude. The planner said it was well received until the next day when the speaker arrived, complaining about her hotel room, the noise next door, and the food, among other things. This was a speaker who talked about not letting the little things impact your attitude, and all she did was complain about the little things. My contact said that she and her staff were put off because this person obviously did not practice what she was paid to preach. This person didn't eat her own crawfish.

Are you a good ambassador of your message? Do you preach customer service but don't promptly return phone calls? Do you promote positive attitude but curse out waiters or demean those who work for you? Do you talk about teamwork but reject input? Do you encourage donating but don't give back in your community? The most successful leaders tend to be the ones whose behavior is consistent, and they are the model for excellence. Simply said, they eat their own crawfish.

Three Ingredients for Killer Crawfish That You Can Eat

1. **A tablespoon of truth.** If you can't take the heat, don't make it so hot. Too many times, we will promise anything to close the sale or pacify the customer. If you can't deliver on what you promise, then don't promise so much. You will always be judged on the margin by which you fail to deliver … and rightly so.

2. **A dash of overdelivery.** Don't just do what you say you are going to do. *Overdo.* The Cajuns have a word, lagniappe, which means "a little bit extra." The difference between good and great is found in the lagniappe.

3. **A heaping helping of atmosphere.** *"Laissez les bons temps rouler*—let the good times roll."* The best way to enjoy crawfish is in a group of people who are drinking beer, dancing, and having a great time. What kind of atmosphere are you creating? People want to buy from, learn from, work with, and do business with those whom they enjoy being around. If you are not reaching your goals, then look at the messenger.

FUN

It's funny how a chubby kid can just be having fun and people call it entertainment.

—Garth Brooks

Pumpkin Pancakes

1½ cups milk
1 egg
2 tablespoons canola oil
1 cup canned pumpkin puree
2 cups all-purpose flour
3 tablespoons brown sugar
1 teaspoon baking soda
1⅛ teaspoon nutmeg
Pinch of ground cloves
½ teaspoon ground cinnamon
½ teaspoon ground ginger
½ teaspoon salt

Mix together the milk, pumpkin puree, egg, and canola oil.
Combine dry ingredients in separate bowl.
Fold wet ingredients into dry until blended.
Pour ⅓ cup of batter onto medium-hot skillet.
When bubbles appear on surface, flip.
Cook for another minute until golden brown.

"If you love what you do what you do for a living, you'll never work a day in your life." If you have ever heard me give a speech, you've heard that quote. Fun works, fun keeps employees engaged, and people want to do business with people who enjoy their jobs.

Musicians join bands for two reasons: it's a great way for average-looking guys to meet girls, and it's a lot of fun. When being in a band stops being fun, bands break up. The same is true for any team, group, organization, or office. When it stops being fun, rewarding, or engaging, people quit (even if they keep on working there). When a culture of fun becomes a priority, an atmosphere of inclusion is created, which in turn builds healthier teams. There is a generational demand for fun in the workplace, and why wouldn't there be? With entertainment being such an integral part of our childhood, why would we not expect and demand an engaging and entertaining work environment as adults? My generation was the last to hear the national anthem before the TV snowed out at midnight. We saw the first VCRs, danced in our living rooms to MTV, and tuned out our parents while turning up our Walkmans. Subsequent generations in the workforce grew up on handheld gaming devices and communicating with texts, pings, pokes, and pics. With decreased attention spans and increased competition for those attention spans, there is a greater need for purposeful engagement and entertainment both at work and with the customer.

I was on a four-hour layover in the Atlanta airport and was looking for something to do. I had grown weary of the book I was reading, all of my e-mails had been answered, my Facebook updates were becoming redundant, and my wife had long ago stopped answering my witty texts with attachments of pictures of odd-looking airport dwellers. I decided that a cup of coffee would help me pass the time, so I set out to find a Starbucks. I arrived at the Starbucks at gate A-16, and I stood in a very long line. I was a little surprised at how many people were working behind the counter, and after a few "how many Starbucks employees does it take to screw in a lightbulb?" jokes had scrolled through my head, I perused the menu. The employees behind the counter were having a great time. They were laughing, joking, and having a lot of fun as they took orders and made coffee.

I heard a voice say, "Hi, how ya doing?"

I turned to see a pleasant young lady talking to me from behind the register. I was a little taken aback as many of us are when we are actually confronted with good customer service, so in my best Joey Tribbiani voice (if you don't know who Joey Tribbiani is, ask a gen Xer), I said, "How you doin'?"

I gave her my order, and she asked my name.

I said, "My name is Patrick."

"Hi, Patrick. Hey, everybody, this is Patrick."

More hellos and smiles from behind the counter. I answered a few questions about my trip and destination, and by the time I received my coffee, I felt like I was saying goodbye to friends. I returned to the Starbucks two more times before my layover was through and finally boarded my plane, jacked up on caffeine and smiles.

Some of the most rewarding and fun jobs I've had have potentially been the most tedious, tiresome, and routine. In hindsight, the reason that I enjoyed them so much was not because of the money I earned but because of the team I worked with. The employees at the gate A-16 Starbucks understood that their job satisfaction was their responsibility. They not only took a mundane job and made it fun, but they also included the customer in on the fun, which made it profitable. When you create an atmosphere of engagement, enjoyment, and inclusion, you create a relationship with the customer or team member that leads to more profits and a stronger team.

COMMUNICATION

Wise men talk because they have something to say;
fools, because they have to say something.

—Plato

Banana Pancakes

1 cup flour
1 tablespoon brown sugar
1 teaspoon baking powder
1/4 teaspoon salt
1 dash cinnamon
2/3 cup soy milk (more if needed)
1/2 banana (very ripe and mashed)
1 teaspoon vanilla

Mix flour, sugar, baking powder, salt, and cinnamon together.
In another bowl, combine all other ingredients.
Combine all ingredients, and stir well.
Add more soy milk if batter is too thick.
Cook on medium-high until bubbles form, and then flip.
Cook for 1 more minute until golden brown.

I recently coached a client in presentation skills, and as a token of appreciation, he sent me a $150 gift card to Ruth's Chris Steak House. My wife and I decided to use it to celebrate our eighth wedding anniversary. I have eaten at Ruth's Chris before and fully intended on tearing through the gift card like Caesar through Gaul, but what happened next was a very expensive lesson in the power of communication. When we arrived at the restaurant, my wife and I requested a booth in the corner so we could be fully present with each other. We ordered wine and perused the menu. I wouldn't call myself cheap, but I have yet to look at the prices on the menu at Ruth's Chris Steak House and not wince ever so slightly. Maybe it was the wine. Maybe it was the mood of the moment, but I decided to throw caution to the wind and order the whole Maine lobster. I love lobster. Some of my fondest childhood memories are of my father returning from business trips to New England with a crate of live Maine lobsters. I can remember being woken up at eleven o' clock one night because my father's plane had been delayed, and that wasn't going to stop us from having a lobster feast. My mother started boiling a pot, and we dined into the wee hours of the morning. That's where my love of lobster began, and now I was continuing it at Ruth's Chris Steak House.

The waiter described the specials, raved about the filet, and finally, I asked, "How's the Maine lobster?"

His eyes lit up as if I'd asked about his children. He went into a description that had me giddy with excitement.

"How much?" I asked. "Thirty-seven dollars? Bring me a Maine lobster."

It was every bit as good as he described. The succulent morsels dissolved in my mouth, the butter dripped from my chin, and my smoking-hot wife stared lovingly at me from across the table. I was in heaven. We enjoyed the evening all the way through the B&B after-dinner drink. When the check arrived, I pulled out my gift card to see if we had fulfilled the limit. We had. Maybe it was intentional, or maybe it was because English was our waiter's second language, but apparently, when I asked how much the lobster was, he left off the words "per pound." I ended up paying $120 for a beady-eyed shellfish! I was speechless. I should have become suspicious when the manager came over to shake my hand and thank me for ordering the lobster. I now know why the kitchen staff was lined up at the door. They were saying goodbye to an old friend. That damned lobster was probably soaking in a tub for years, growing fat, waiting for a sucker like me to come along.

What would you do if you were in that situation? I am not afraid to express myself when I feel taken advantage of, but in this case, I didn't complain, and I didn't cause a scene. I simply paid the bill, tipped the waiter well, and left with my wife. I figure the lack of communication was as much my fault as it was Raul's. Will I go back to Ruth's Chris? Probably, although that particular restaurant has seen the last of me. There are two parts to effectively communicating. Listening is as important as speaking. My fault was in my assumption and not asking questions. His fault was not presenting all of the facts. Did Raul benefit from the lack of communication?

Yes and no. He made about thirty dollars more on his tip, but he lost the opportunity to create a profitable relationship. Every time you interact with a customer, it is an opportunity to seed the relationship. Had Raul been more forthcoming with the information, he would have created an emotional debt that I would have paid at a future date, maybe with friends, clients, or a party of ten. Are you clear with your team about the importance of communication? Have you created a culture of open communication with protocols and best practices? When dealing with customers, poor communication can cause more than stress; it can cost you in profits.

I don't much care for awards shows. Every now and then, however, I will see someone on an awards show who impresses or even inspires me. I was inspired when Cuba Gooding Jr. won an Oscar for his role in *Jerry Maguire* and when Roberto Benigni won an Oscar for his 1998 film, *Life is Beautiful*. I usually just see a room full of people who haven't had a job in months who are just happy to be dressed up and out of the house. My wife enjoys awards shows, so when the Oscars, Tonys, or SAG Awards roll around, we usually find ourselves curled up on the couch in front of the TV. I rarely recall the winners, but there was one show in particular that stands out in my mind. It was the 2010 Screen Actors Guild Awards show. I was quite impressed with Sandra Bullock and especially Betty White, who hails back to an era where class and decorum were the order of the day. I, however, was completely underwhelmed by Drew Barrymore. When the award for best actress in a television movie or miniseries was announced, Drew Barrymore's name was called. She gave the customary "oh my God, I can't believe it's me" look to her fellow aisle mates and then made the triumphant march to the stage to accept her prize. This is where the wheels came off.

I am a professional speaker. I believe that a person's ability to effectively communicate thoughts, ideas, and gratitude is paramount in fomenting success, regardless of profession. Apparently, Drew Barrymore doesn't think so. As she accepted her award, she began to stutter and stumble over her words in a cutesy and contrived display of ums and ands. When the awkward moment began to turn uncomfortable, she said, "Usually improv is a good thing. It's backfiring on me very badly right now." I have news for you, Drew; it's not improv … *it's a speech!* Considering that you have been in the movie business since before ET phoned home, it is a speech that you should have been prepared for! In a matter of seconds, she went, in my eyes, from brilliance to buffoonery, from star to stammerer, from "Bless my stars" to "Bless her heart," all because she was painfully unprepared.

There are certain moments where the right words delivered with eloquence, passion, and skill can create a mountaintop experience. In sales and customer service, these moments happen *every day*. Are you prepared? Have you developed the skill and "material" to inspire people to action?

Three Ways to Prepare For Your Awards Speech

1. **Collect material.** Continually be on the lookout for real-life experiences, stories, and anecdotes that can be recalled and delivered with

dexterity at a moment's notice. Become an expert in your field and your clients' by reading books, articles, and web copy about topics that relate to the field. Keep a file.

2. **Listen to great speakers.** Never miss an opportunity to listen to great speakers speak. Don't steal their material; take note of their styles and techniques and then create your own. TED talks are great for this. Even though most are not professional speakers, many are amazing.

3. **Practice.** As good as you think you are, *you're not!* I don't care how many successful wedding toasts you've given. Until you've delivered a thousand speeches or presentations, you still have room for improvement. Even then, you still can find ways to become better. Join Toastmasters ... *now!*

CONTEXT

No object is so beautiful that, under certain condi-tions, it will not look ugly.

—Oscar Wilde
(I believe the reverse is also true)

Eggnog Pancakes

Follow directions for Old-Fashioned Pancakes.
Substitute eggnog for milk.
Add a little nutmeg to the dry ingredients.

In 2004, my world changed. It was altered not because of events or circumstances but because of context. I became a husband in 2004. I became a father in 2004, again in 2005, and once more in 2008. Finally, my wife told me that if I wanted another child, I would have to do it with my next wife. Up until then, my identity existed on the basis of accomplishment, achievement, or circumstance, but I suddenly found myself with an identity predicated by something different: context. John Crudele, my buddy and fellow professional speaker, summed up the true meaning of context. He told me that the moon is only the moon because of the earth. Its relationship to the earth is what creates its identity. He said that without context and mutual attraction, it is just a rock floating in space. I am a husband and father not because of me or what I do but because of my relationship to my wife and children. Just like our identity as a family member is determined by the relationship with the other members of the family, so is our relationship to the customer. Our customers are not our customers because we exist. We are who we are because our customers exist. As a professional speaker and writer, I only maintain that identity if I have an audience. If not, I am just another opinionated big mouth looking at an empty calendar on the wall of my office. I am a humorist. I believe that funny is funner, so I try to incorporate humor into everything I do. I was once asked during an interview, "What is the difference between a comedian and a humorist?" I thought for a minute about all of the humorists that I know and gave the most honest answer I could, even though many comedians would disagree. I said that most comedians believe the audience is there for them. As a humorist, I am there for my audience. When you treat your customers as if your existence depends on them, you will be nicer, more efficient, more transparent, and just plain better than if you operate as if your customers need you. When your customer relationship is based on mutual attraction and context, you decommoditize your position in the market and become the brand. Branding is more than selling. We all have a brand. You can easily substitute student, employee, or teammate for customer.

Staring at the painting of the two Japanese women, I realized that I have stared at that picture—now hanging in my mother's house—my whole life. I first remember it on a wall in my grandparents' house beside the upright piano that my grandfather loved to play, especially after a scotch on the rocks had loosened his fingers. Surrounded by Southwestern art, a shadow box of arrowheads, and a painting of a running mule deer, I didn't understand how out of place the painting of the two Japanese women was. I just knew that it was always there and had come to represent the dependable, unchanging stability that tends to only be found at your grandparents' house. As a child, I knew that my grandfather had fought in World War II, but his service had been somewhat marginalized in my young mind by what I saw in old movies and what little he told me about his experience. To me, WWII was a bunch of white guys wearing green or khaki uniforms, with shirts tucked in and hair like my hundreds of plastic army men, no one actually got hurt, and everyone got to go home for dinner. It wasn't until I had left my teenage years behind that I actually learned the truth about World War II and the truth about the painting.

If you study the painting in my mother's house, you may think it is good. You may even think it is really good despite the simplicity of the subjects. How much would you pay for a good painting—$200, $500, or $1,000? If you were to compare it to a similar painting, you may decide that it doesn't measure up. You may even begin to notice the rudimentary flaws in the design, the disproportional features of the subjects, and perhaps the fallibility of the artist. You may decide that it isn't worth a lot of money until you hear, as Paul Harvey used to say, "the rest of the story."

My grandfather was an engineer in the US Army Air Corps during World War II. He built runways and buildings on Okinawa. One of his responsibilities was to oversee Japanese POWs. I've heard horror stories of how the American POWs in the South Pacific were treated. My grandfather, although efficient and strict, treated the POWs he supervised with kindness, and allowed no ill treatment on his watch. As a matter of fact, because of the humane treatment that the Japanese POWs received under my grandfather, they viewed him with respect. I was told that the Japanese soldiers put on theatrical productions and invited him and his officers to attend. They cleared the front row to provide them a place to sit. When my grandfather was due to return to the United States, he bid farewell to many of the Japanese POWs that he had come to know and, in some cases, like. It was then that he was unexpectedly presented with a gift.

You may look at the painting of the two Japanese women hanging on the wall in my mother's house and think it is good. You may even decide you would pay $200, $500, or even $1,000 dollars for such a painting. The value of the painting, however, may change in your mind if you knew that in 1945, a Japanese prisoner of war painted two Japanese women on a United States Army–issued bedsheet, using paints that he made with materials that he found in and around an Okinawan POW camp. He then presented the painting to my grandfather as a token of appreciation for the kindness bestowed upon him and his comrades by their captor. How about now—$1 million, $2 million? How much would someone pay for a painting with the history of the one on my mother's wall? That is a question that will never be answered because the painting will never be sold.

Beauty is in the eye of the beholder. Value is in the eye of the buyer. Long-term relationships are created when value is provided. We routinely pay four dollars for a cup of Starbucks coffee—not because it tastes better than the coffee sold in the gas station or at McDonald's but rather because of the context in which it is delivered. Why do people pay hundreds of dollars more for front-row seats at a Broadway show or rock concert? Context! Creating an extraordinary customer experience is not simply about providing quality goods and services. It is about providing those goods and services within the context of these four things:

1. **Friendship.** People will buy from friends first.
2. **Trust.** When your goal is to provide value rather than simply closing a sale, then you establish trust.
3. **Convenience.** Is it easy to do business with you? Your customers will tell you.
4. **Empathy.** People want to buy from those who genuinely care about their challenges and problems. When you care, you become a guide to the solution.

Whether you are an entrepreneur or in sales, management, or education, the product, service, or message that you provide is only as powerful as the person behind the product and the context in which it is delivered.

COMMUNITY

It takes a village to raise a child.

—African proverb

Brown Sugar-Oatmeal Pancakes

1¼ rolled oats
1½ cups wheat flour
1 cup all-purpose flour
¼ teaspoon baking soda
1 teaspoon salt
⅔ cup packed brown sugar
2 eggs (beaten)
4 tablespoons vegetable oil
2 cups buttermilk
1 teaspoon vanilla

In large mixing bowl, whisk together dry ingredients,
except brown sugar.
In another bowl, whisk egg, brown sugar, milk, oil, and vanilla.
Pour ⅓ cups of batter on heated skillet.
Turn when bubbles form, and cook a minute longer.

"I'm with the band." Four powerful words. Four words that can circumvent lines, bypass security, procure free drinks, and even gain a little companionship. The only four words that supersede "I'm with the band" are "I'm *in* the band," and when I was *in* the band, my band, Almost Amos, used to play at the Treasure Bay casino in Biloxi, Mississippi, from time to time. When we played Treasure Bay, we would get booked for a week at a time, and since we played every night for six nights, we got to know many of the patrons. One night after a show, one of the regulars approached me and said, "Y'all are our favorite band." I asked why, and he told me that it made him feel good when he walked in the room and I acknowledged him from the stage. He taught me that people want to feel like they are with the band, and even a simple nod of the head will create that feeling of inclusion. As I mentioned in a previous chapter, when you create inclusion, people will want to buy from you, learn from you, work hard for you, and love you. You will increase sales, grow profits, and maximize productivity. We tend to create that feeling of inclusion in our lives by aligning ourselves with communities. This is why we go to church, join clubs, play on teams, participate in political parties, and join causes. In Jeff Jarvis's book *What Would Google Do?*, he tells the story of the 2006 World Economic Forum in Davos, Switzerland. The forum was the convergence of some of the most brilliant minds in business, politics, journalism, and academia. In 2006, social media had just begun to creep into the consciousness of those of us over thirty years of age, and companies were trying to find ways to monetize it. Jarvis reports that a big newspaper publisher was grilling twenty-two-year-old Mark Zuckerberg, the wunderkind creator of Facebook, about online communities.

The reporter desperately asked Zuckerberg, "How do we own an online community like you have?"

Zuckerberg is reported to have simply looked at him with his geeky grin and said, "You can't."

He later went on to explain that you don't create online communities; they already exist. If you can help them do what they do better, you create elegant organization. Isn't this why we join communities in the first place? We join a church because we feel good being around like-minded people, and we feel that we become better people by being a part of that community. We create communities based on interests, vocation, or avocation. I am a part of the National Speakers Association because I believe that everyone should be a part of his or her industry trade association. I can say in good conscience that every positive thing that has happened to me in the speaking business has been a direct or indirect result of a relationship that I created in NSA. The National Speakers Association is one of my communities, and I am better because of it.

My father was a builder of community. He was one of those people who simply made you feel good by being around him. He was an encourager and used to go to great lengths to help others succeed, which, I believe, was a major factor in his success. He believed in Zig Ziglar's philosophy: "You can get everything in life that you want if you help enough people get what they want." My father was a big man, and he consistently greeted my brother and me in the same way. He would wrap his arms around us, kiss us right on the lips, and say, "Oh, son, do you know how much your daddy loves you?" Waking up in the morning, coming home from school, or seeing him for the first time after a business trip, he would run up to me and my brother, scoop us up in his arms, plant a scratchy kiss on us, and say ,"Oh, son, do you know how much your daddy loves you?" That's cool when you are five, but when you are fifteen years old and just coming off of the wrestling mat after having just lost the match by two points, only to see him walking across the gym with arms wide … not so cool. That was just the way he was. He had no problem showing the people in his life how much they meant to him.

My father died in 2001. If you have lost someone important in your life, then you may agree that regardless of how long ago they passed, it can seem just like yesterday. My father's death was the most impactful event in my life. I've heard it said that a boy doesn't truly become a man until he loses his father. If that is true, then I became a man at the age of thirty. I felt lost, uncertain, and unready to face the world without the safety net of those big arms and that scratchy kiss telling me that everything would be okay. As I've told this story across the country, I've heard similar expressions of emotion from those who have also lost someone close to them. I realize that this experience does not make us unique, but what we learn from this experience does. The worst day was not the day that Dad died; it was the day we found out he was not going to live. His liver was failing, and the transplant list was long. We learned that, because of a growing lesion on his liver, a transplant was no longer an option, so I packed my bags, put my guitar away, and moved back home to Auburn, Alabama. My brother came in on the weekends, and we spent time together as a family. We cried a lot, we laughed a lot, and we planned for life without Dad. He got to participate in the planning, and we feel fortunate for that. As my father and I sat on our deck in Auburn, Alabama, I realized that, as sad as we were, I was looking at a grateful man. My father knew he was at the end of his life, and he was not regretting that he didn't have a bigger house or more stuff, but he was instead grateful for the relationships in his life. He had a family that loved him without measure, and he had friends and colleagues that loved and respected him as well. As I mentioned, my dad was a builder of community, and when word got out that he was ill, his communities responded vigorously. First and foremost, his intimate circle of family and friends came to be with him. They talked with him, cried with him, prayed with him, and even slept by his side. Our community of Auburn, Alabama, wrapped its arms around our family and held us close. There was not a day that passed that we were not met at the door by a casserole, pasta salad, or baked ham. One good thing about dying in the South is you don't have to worry about how much butter, sugar, and fat is in the recipe. My father was a professional speaker and humorist, and he was an early member of the National Speakers Association. We were lifted immensely by the response of our friends in NSA. His funeral was attended by eighteen past national presidents, along with numerous other NSA members who went to huge efforts to be there. One individual in particular flew from California and came to the funeral, only to catch a return flight that same day. They told stories about how my dad had impacted their lives and that they wanted to be there at the end. Wow! What a testament to the power of community.

On the day that Dad died, we knew the end was near. He had been unresponsive for a couple of weeks, and we had moved him to a hospice facility in Auburn. Early that morning, a nurse called and told us that if we wanted to be there when he died, we had better come now. We all rushed to Dad's bedside and were met by our preacher and a few friends. We all gathered around his bed, holding hands, singing, and saying prayers. As I stood there in that small room, looking at my hero, my mentor, my friend, I felt compelled to lean over, wrap my big arms around him, give him a scratchy kiss, and say, "Oh, Daddy, do you know how much I love you?" He died ten minutes later but not before his lips slowly raised in one last kiss.

Watching my father pass taught me how important it is to create community in our lives. First and foremost, I am vigorously present with my wife and children. I will consider myself a monumental failure if I let a day go by where I don't grab them in my arms, give them a scratchy kiss, and tell them how much I love them. I also vowed to not only embrace the community in which I live but to also create community in my professional life as well. We spend a lot of time with the people at work. Those relationships are valuable, and although I recommend you leave the kissing at home, your professional relationships are a community that should be nurtured.

What about you? If you were to die next week, who would rush to be by your side? If you can't point to people outside of your immediate friends and family, then I suggest that you become more engaged in your communities. My next-door neighbor Bob died not long after we moved in next door. Although I didn't know him well, I was at his funeral, and as I listened to the eulogy, I realized in one sentence why Bob Smith was such a big part of our community. The preacher said that whenever there was work to be done, Bob would simply say, "Give me the heavy end." If you are serious about growing in your profession, your life, or your community, be willing to take the heavy end, and your customers, clients, coworkers, and family will respond with vigor and enthusiasm.

How to Create Community

1. **Join your trade association.** This is an opportunity to grow, learn, and create relationships with the top producers of your industry.

2. **Create unique engagement in your hometown.** Westcott Automotive is a successful car dealership in our area. Every Christmas, you can bring toys to the dealership to be assembled free of charge. The salesmen cheerfully put the toys together so dads won't have to sneak off and do it Christmas Eve. Who do you think we go to when it is time to buy new car?

3. **Be an encourager.** This is the easiest way to create community. When you make a habit out of making others feel special and helping them achieve their goals, you will create a culture of kindness, inclusion, and excellence.

FINAL THOUGHT

Everybody is in sales. We all have customers. For the purposes of this book, I define customers as people to whom we sell, teach, preach, work with, serve, or cater to. We are our own best and most important customers. Although the purpose of this book is to make your customers flip for you, it is also about creating excellence in your life. People want to buy from happy, healthy, prosperous, people. If you incorporate these ideas into your life, you will not only create extraordinary customers relationships, but you will create a life of abundance where the odds are certainly *stacked* in your favor.

CPSIA information can be obtained
at www.ICGtesting.com
Printed in the USA
FFOW01n1819100615
14025FF

9 781457 515798